Victorian Poets
and
Prose Writers

GOLDENTREE BIBLIOGRAPHIES

In Language and Literature
under the series editorship of
O. B. Hardison, Jr.

Victorian Poets
and
Prose Writers

SECOND EDITION

compiled by

Jerome H. Buckley

Harvard University

AHM Publishing Corporation
ARLINGTON HEIGHTS, ILLINOIS 60004

ISBN: 0-88295-560-8, paper
ISBN: 0-88295-567-5, cloth

Library of Congress Card Number: 76-5212

PRINTED IN THE UNITED STATES OF AMERICA

787

Contents

      The entries under individual writers are generally
      arranged in the following sub-categories:
         EDITIONS (By order of general collections
            to more specific works)
         BIOGRAPHY
         CRITICISM

CONTENTS

Preface

The following bibliography is intended for graduate and advanced undergraduate students in courses on Victorian literature and related subjects. A convenient guide to scholarship in the field, it lists thirty-two Victorian poets and prose writers: all of the major figures and a substantial representation of the lesser ones. Though this second edition considerably expands the 1966 edition (material through 1974 and early 1975 is now included), it is still necessarily selective. It aspires to usefulness within manageable compass rather than completeness. It places primary emphasis on relatively recent scholarship and criticism. It excludes writers and works of fiction, except insofar as such authors—Kipling, Stevenson, Hardy, and Pater—are otherwise known as masters of verse or the essay. Victorian fiction is treated in a separate Goldentree Bibliography, Ian Watt, *The British Novel: Scott Through Hardy*.

Sources of further bibliographical information are indicated under "General Studies" and frequently under the "Criticism" of specific authors. The references generally omitted from the present listings fall into several classes:

Unpublished M.A. and Ph.D. theses and dissertations.

Articles and specialized monographs in languages other than English—though key books in French, such as Bonnerot's biography of Arnold, are included.

Late Victorian and early twentieth-century essays, if they have been effectively superseded by later studies.

In general, the compiler has sought to steer a middle course between the brief lists of references included in the average textbook and the long professional bibliographies in which significant items are often lost in the sheer number of citations. This bibliography should materially assist the student in his or her effort to survey a topic, write reports and term papers, prepare for examinations, and do independent reading. Attention is called to several features intended to enhance its utility:

(1) Extra margin on each page permits listing of library call numbers of often used items.

(2) Extra space at the bottom of each page permits the inclusion of additional entries.

(3) The authors are arranged alphabetically, and the entries are numbered consecutively throughout the book for ready cross-reference.

(4) An index by author follows the bibliography proper.

Additional details accompany some of the entries. A very few items, usually not more than one or two for an author, are asterisked as those which the compiler regards as the best established general studies in a given area or the most useful broad interpretations of an author's life or work. The numbers in boldface provide cross-reference to titles listed elsewhere in full. Descriptive phrases help define or evaluate some of the more opaque titles. Though many paperbacks do not remain long in print, an effort has been made to indicate some of the best paperback editions available in recent years, the series numbers of which appear as in *Paperbound Books in Print*.

In preparing the revision of this bibliography, the compiler is indebted to many Victorianists for emendations and helpful advice. He will welcome suggestions for future editions.

The Social and Political Background

1 BENTLEY, Nicholas. *The Victorian Scene: A Picture Book of the Period, 1837–1901*. Greenwich, Conn.: New York Graphic Society, 1969.

2 BEST, Geoffrey. *Mid-Victorian Britain, 1851–1875*. New York: Schocken Books, 1972.*

3 BETJEMAN, John, ed. *Victorian and Edwardian London from Old Photographs*. New York: Viking, 1969.

4 BOLITHO, Hector. *Albert, Prince Consort*. London: Parrish, 1964.

5 BRIGGS, Asa. *The Age of Improvement*. New York: Oxford University Press, 1962.*

6 BRIGGS, Asa. *Victorian Cities*. London: Oldhams, 1963.

7 BRIGGS, Asa, ed. *The Nineteenth Century*. New York: McGraw-Hill, 1970.

8 BRINTON, Crane. *English Political Thought in the Nineteenth Century*. Cambridge: Harvard University Press, 1949.*

9 BRYANT, Arthur. *The Pageant of England, 1840–1940*. New York: Harper, 1941.

10 BURN, W. L. *The Age of Equipoise: A Study of the Mid-Victorian Generation*. New York: Norton, 1964.*

11 BURROW, J. W. *Evolution and Society: A Study in Victorian Social Theory*. New York: Cambridge University Press, 1966.

12 DYOS, H. J., and Michael WOLFF, eds. *The Victorian City: Images and Realities*, 2 vols. London: Routledge Kegan Paul, 1973.*

13 ENSOR, R. C. K. *England, 1870–1914*. London: Oxford University Press, 1936.*

14 EVANS, Joan. *The Victorians*. London: Cambridge University Press, 1966.

15 FAY, C. R. *Life and Labour in the Nineteenth Century*. Cambridge: Cambridge University Press, 1947.

16 HALÉVY, Elie. *History of the English People in the Nineteenth Century*, 6 vols. London: Benn, 1949–1952.*

17 HARRISON, Brian. *Drink and the Victorians: The Temperance Question in England, 1815–1872*. London: Faber, 1971.

18 HARRISON, J. F. C. *The Early Victorians, 1832–1861*. New York: Praeger, 1971.

19 INGE, W. R. *The Victorian Age*. Cambridge: Cambridge University Press, 1922.

20 KITSON CLARK, G. *The Making of Victorian England*. Cambridge: Harvard University Press, 1962.*

21 LONGFORD, Elizabeth. *Queen Victoria: Born to Succeed*. New York: Harper & Row, 1964.

1

THE SOCIAL AND POLITICAL BACKGROUND

22 McCARTHY, Justin. *A History of Our Own Times*, 5 vols. New York: Harper, 1905.

23 MONYPENNY, W. F., and G. E. BUCKLE. *The Life of Benjamin Disraeli, Earl of Beaconsfield*, 2 vols. New York: Macmillan, 1929.

24 MORLEY, John. *The Life of William Ewart Gladstone*, 3 vols. New York: Macmillan, 1903.

25 STRACHEY, Lytton. *Eminent Victorians*. London: Chatto and Windus, 1918. [Also issued as a Capricorn paperback.]

26 STRACHEY, Lytton. *Queen Victoria*. New York: Harcourt Brace, 1921.

27 THOMSON, David. *England in the Nineteenth Century*. London: Penguin Books, 1950.

28 TREVELYAN, G. M. *British History in the Nineteenth Century, and After, 1782–1919*. London: Longmans, 1938.

29 WHITE, R. J. *From Peterloo to the Crystal Palace*. London: Heinemann, 1972.

30 WINGFIELD-STRATFORD, Esmé Cecil. *The Victorian Cycle*. New York: Morrow, 1935.

31 WOOD, Anthony. *Nineteenth Century Britain*. London: Longmans, 1960.

32 WOODWARD, E. L. *The Age of Reform, 1815–1870*. London: Oxford University Press, 1962.*

33 YOUNG, G. M., ed. *Victorian England*. New York: Oxford University Press, 1953.*

34 YOUNG, G. M. *Victorian England: Portrait of an Age*. New York: Oxford University Press, 1936.*

General Studies in Intellectual and Literary History

35 ALTICK, Richard D. *The English Common Reader: A Social History of the Mass Reading Public, 1800–1900*. Chicago: University of Chicago Press, 1957.*

36 ALTICK, Richard D., and William R. MATTHEWS, comps. *Guide to Doctoral Dissertations in Victorian Literature, 1886–1958*. Urbana: University of Illinois Press, 1960.

37 ALTICK, Richard D. *Victorian People and Ideas*. New York: Norton, 1973. [A useful guide to the social and intellectual background.]

38 APPLEMAN, Philip, *et al.*, eds. *1859: Entering an Age of Crisis*. Bloomington: Indiana University Press, 1959.

38 ARMSTRONG, Isobel, ed. *The Major Victorian Poets: Reconsiderations*. Lincoln: University of Nebraska Press, 1969. [Modern critical essays.]

40 ASLIN, Elizabeth. *The Aesthetic Movement: Prelude to Art Nouveau*. New York: Praeger, 1969.

41 BALL, Patricia M. *The Central Self: A Study in Romantic and Victorian Imagination*. London: Athlone Press, 1969.

42 BARILLI, Renato, ed. *I Prerafaelliti*. Milan: Fratelli Fabbri, 1969. [A good Pre-Raphaelite picture book.]

43 BATESON, F. W., ed. *Cambridge Bibliography of English Literature*, 3 vols., vol. III. Cambridge: Cambridge University Press, 1940.

44 BATHO, Edith, and Bonamy DOBRÉE, eds. *The Victorians and After, 1830–1914*. New York: Dover, 1952.

45 BEACH, Joseph Warren. *The Concept of Nature in Nineteenth-Century Poetry*. New York: Macmillan, 1936.

46 BENZIGER, James. *Images of Eternity: Studies in the Poetry of Religious Vision from Wordsworth to T. S. Eliot*. Carbondale: Southern Illinois University Press, 1963.

47 BLOOM, Harold. *Ringers in the Tower: Studies in Romantic Tradition*. Chicago: University of Chicago Press, 1971. [Includes discussions of Tennyson, Browning, Ruskin, Pater.]

48 BOWEN, Desmond. *The Idea of the Victorian Church: The Role of the Church of England in State and Society*. Montreal: McGill University Press, 1968.

49 BRADBURY, Malcolm, and David PALMER, eds. *Victorian Poetry*. London: Arnold, 1972. [Stratford-upon-Avon Series 15; modern essays. Also paperback.]

50 BROWN, Alan W. *The Metaphysical Society: Victorian Minds in Crisis, 1869–1880*. New York: Columbia University Press, 1947.

51 BUCKLEY, Jerome H. "General Materials." [Review of research.] See **81**.

52 BUCKLEY, Jerome H. *The Triumph of Time: A Study of the Victorian Concepts of Time, History, Progress, and Decadence*. Cambridge: Harvard University Press, 1966.

GENERAL STUDIES

53 BUCKLEY, Jerome H. *The Victorian Temper: A Study in Literary Culture.* Cambridge: Harvard University Press, 1951, 1969. [Reissued by Vintage Books, V259.]*

54 BURDETT, Osbert. *The Beardsley Period.* London: Lane, 1925.

55 BUSH, Douglas. *Mythology and the Romantic Tradition in English Poetry.* Cambridge: Harvard University Press, 1937. [Reissued as a Norton paperback.]*

56 BUSH, Douglas. *Science and English Poetry.* New York: Oxford University Press, 1950.

57 CARTER, John, and Graham POLLARD. *An Enquiry into the Nature of Certain Nineteenth Century Pamphlets.* New York: Scribner, 1934. [On forged "first" editions of the Victorian poets.]

58 CHADWICK, Owen. *The Victorian Church,* 2 parts. New York: Oxford University Press, 1966, 1970.*

59 CHANDLER, Alice. *A Dream of Order: The Medieval Ideal in Nineteenth-Century English Literature.* Lincoln: University of Nebraska Press, 1970.

60 CHARLESWORTH, Barbara. *Dark Passages: The Decadent Consciousness in Victorian Literature.* Madison: University of Wisconsin Press, 1965.

61 CHESTERTON, G. K. *The Victorian Age in Literature.* New York: Holt, 1913. [Reissued as a Notre Dame paperback.]

62 CHURCH, Richard W. *The Oxford Movement.* London: Macmillan, 1894.

63 COCKSHUT, A. O. J. *The Unbelievers: English Agnostic Thought, 1840–1890.* London: Collins, 1964.

64 COOKE, J. D., and Lionel STEVENSON. *English Literature of the Victorian Period.* New York: Appleton-Century-Crofts, 1949.

65 CRUSE, Amy. *The Victorians and Their Reading.* Boston: Houghton Mifflin, 1936.

66 DAICHES, David. *Some Late Victorian Attitudes.* New York: Norton, 1969.

67 DE LA MARE, Walter, ed. *The Eighteen-Eighties.* Cambridge: Cambridge University Press, 1930.

68 DE LAURA, David J., ed. *Victorian Prose: A Guide to Research.* New York: Modern Language Association of America, 1973. [Treats all the prose writers listed below except Darwin. Useful chapters on intellectual history. Paperback.]*

69 DODDS, John W. *The Age of Paradox: A Biography of England, 1841–1851.* New York: Rinehart, 1952.

70 DRINKWATER, John, ed. *The Eighteen-Sixties.* Cambridge: Cambridge University Press, 1932.

71 DRINKWATER, John. *Victorian Poetry.* New York: Doran, 1924.

72 EHRSAM, T. G., R. H. DEILY, and R. M. SMITH, comps. *Bibliographies of Twelve Victorian Authors.* New York: Wilson, 1936.

73 ELLIOTT-BINNS, L. E. *Religion in the Victorian Era.* Greenwich, Conn.: Seabury Press, 1953.

74 ELLIS, S. M. *Mainly Victorian.* London: Hutchinson, 1925.

75 ELTON, Oliver. *A Survey of English Literature, 1780–1880,* 4 vols. New York: Macmillan, 1920.

76 ELWIN, Malcolm. *Old Gods Falling.* London: Collins, 1939.

77 EVANS, B. I. *English Poetry in the Later Nineteenth Century.* London: Methuen, 1933.

4

GENERAL STUDIES

78 FAIRCHILD, Hoxie N. *Religious Trends in English Poetry*, vol. IV, 1830–1880; vol. V, 1880–1920. New York: Columbia University Press, 1957, 1962.

79 FAIRWEATHER, Eugene R., ed. *The Oxford Movement*. London: Oxford University Press, 1964. [A source book of documents.]

80 FARMER, A. J. *Le Mouvement esthétique et décadent en Angleterre*. Paris: Champion, 1931.

81 FAVERTY, Frederic E., ed. *The Victorian Poets: A Guide to Research*. Cambridge: Harvard University Press, 1968. [Treats all of the poets listed below, except Lear, Gilbert, and Lewis Carroll.]*

82 FOAKES, R. A. *The Romantic Assertion: A Study of the Language of Nineteenth Century Poetry*. New Haven: Yale University Press, 1958.

83 FORD, George H. *Keats and the Victorians*. New Haven: Yale University Press, 1944, 1962.

84 FOXELL, Nigel. *Ten Poems Analysed*. Oxford: Pergamon Press, 1966. [Includes discussions of "Lady of Shalott," "A Grammarian's Funeral," "Wreck of the *Deutschland*."]

85 GAUNT, William. *The Aesthetic Adventure*. New York: Harcourt Brace, 1945.

86 GAUNT, William. *The Pre-Raphaelite Tragedy*. London: Cape, 1942.

87 GRANVILLE-BARKER, Harley, ed. *The Eighteen-Seventies*. Cambridge: Cambridge University Press, 1929.

88 GRIERSON, H. J. C. *Lyrical Poetry from Blake to Hardy*. New York: Harcourt Brace, 1929.

89 GROSS, John. *The Rise and Fall of the Man of Letters*. New York: Macmillan, 1969.

90 HEARN, Lafcadio. *Pre-Raphaelite and Other Poets*. New York: Dodd Mead, 1922.

91 HICKS, Granville. *Figures of Transition: A Study of British Literature at the End of the Nineteenth Century*. New York: Macmillan, 1939.

92 HILTON, Timothy. *The Pre-Raphaelites*. London: Thames and Hudson, 1970.

93 HOLLOWAY, John. *The Victorian Sage: Studies in Argument*. London: Macmillan, 1953. [Discusses Carlyle, Disraeli, George Eliot, Newman, Arnold, Hardy. Reissued as a Norton paperback.]*

94 HOUGH, Graham. *The Last Romantics*. London: Duckworth, 1949. [Reissued as a Barnes and Noble paperback.]

95 HOUGHTON, Walter E. *The Victorian Frame of Mind, 1830–1870*. New Haven: Yale University Press, 1957. [Also a Yale paperback.]*

96 HOUGHTON, Walter E., ed. *The Wellesley Index to Victorian Periodicals*, in progress. Toronto: University of Toronto Press, 1966, 1972.*

97 JACKSON, Holbrook. *The Eighteen Nineties*. New York: Knopf, 1922.

98 JOHNSON, E. D. H. *The Alien Vision of Victorian Poetry*. Princeton: Princeton University Press, 1952.

99 KERMODE, Frank. *Romantic Image*. London: Routledge Kegan Paul, 1957.

100 LANGBAUM, Robert, ed. *The Victorian Age*. New York: Fawcett, 1967. [Critical essays. Fawcett Premier paperback.]

101 LESTER, John A., Jr. *Journey Through Despair, 1880–1914: Transformations in British Literary Culture*. Princeton: Princeton University Press, 1968.

102 LEVINE, George, ed. *The Emergence of Victorian Consciousness*. New York: The Free Press, 1966.

GENERAL STUDIES

103 LEVINE, George, and William A. MADDEN, eds. *The Art of Victorian Prose.* New York: Oxford University Press, 1968. [Essays on Mill, Arnold, Carlyle, Macaulay, Darwin, Ruskin, Pater, and prose style generally.]

104 LEVINE, Richard A., ed. *Backgrounds to Victorian Literature.* San Francisco: Chandler, 1967. [Essays in social and intellectual history.]

105 LIPPINCOTT, B. E. *Victorian Critics of Democracy.* Minneapolis: University of Minnesota Press, 1938.

106 LISTER, Raymond. *Victorian Narrative Paintings.* New York: Potter, 1966.

107 LUCAS, F. L. *Ten Victorian Poets.* New York: Macmillan, 1948. (Essays on all the more important poets except Hopkins).

108 LUCAS, John, ed. *Literature and Politics in the Nineteenth Century.* New York: Barnes and Noble, 1971.

109 MAAS, Jeremy. *Victorian Painters.* New York: Putnam, 1969.

110 MADDEN, William A. "The Victorian Sensibility." *Victorian Studies,* VII (1963), 67–97.

111 MANDELBAUM, Maurice. *History, Man, and Reason: A Study in Nineteenth-Century Thought.* Baltimore: Johns Hopkins Press, 1971.

112 MASSINGHAM, H. J., and Hugh MASSINGHAM, eds. *The Great Victorians.* London: Nicholson and Watson, 1932.

113 MERIVALE, Patricia. *Pan the Goat-God: His Myth in Modern Times,* Chap. III, "Victorian Pan." Cambridge: Harvard University Press, 1969.

114 METZ, R. *A Hundred years of British Philosophy.* New York: Macmillan, 1938.

115 MILLER, J. Hillis. *The Disappearance of God: Five Nineteenth Century Writers.* Cambridge: Harvard University Press, 1963. [On De Quincey, Browning, Arnold, Emily Brontë, Hopkins.]*

116 MIYOSHI, Masao. *The Divided Self: A Perspective on the Literature of the Victorians.* New York: New York University Press, 1969. [Also paperback.]

117 MOERS, Ellen. *The Dandy: Brummell to Beerbohm.* New York: Viking, 1960.

118 NEFF, Emery E. *A Revolution in European Poetry.* New York: Columbia University Press, 1940.

119 NELSON, James G. *The Sublime Puritan: Milton and the Victorians.* Madison: University of Wisconsin Press, 1963.

120 PECKHAM, Morse. *Beyond the Tragic Vision: The Quest for Identity in the Nineteenth Century.* New York: Braziller, 1962.

121 PETERS, Robert L. "Whistler and the English Poets of the 1890's." *Modern Language Quarterly,* XVIII (1957), 251–261.

122 PINTO, Vivian de Sola. *Crisis in English Poetry, 1880–1940.* New York: Longmans, 1951.

123 PREYER, Robert O., ed. *Victorian Literature: Selected Essays.* New York: Harper and Row, 1967. [Modern critical essays. Harper Torchbook.]

124 ROPPEN, Georg. *Evolution and Poetic Belief.* Oxford: Blackwell, 1956.

125 ROSENBLATT, Louise M. *L'Idée de l'art pour l'art dans la littérature anglaise pendant la période victorienne.* Paris: Champion, 1931.

126 ROUTH, H. V. *Towards the Twentieth Century.* New York: Macmillan, 1937.

127 RUDMAN, Harry W. *Italian Nationalism and English Letters.* New York: Columbia University Press, 1940.

GENERAL STUDIES

128 RYALS, Clyde de L., ed. *Nineteenth-Century Literary Perspectives: Essays in Honor of Lionel Stevenson*. Durham, N.C.: Duke University Press, 1974. [Includes essays on Victorian poets.]

129 SAINTSBURY, George. *A History of Nineteenth Century Literature*. London: Macmillan, 1896.

130 SAINTSBURY, George. *The Later Nineteenth Century*. Edinburgh: Blackwood, 1907.

131 SAN JUAN, Epifanio, Jr. "Toward a Definition of Victorian Activism." *Studies in English Literature*, IV (1964), 583–600.

132 SCHNEEWIND, J. B. *Backgrounds of Victorian Literature*. New York: Random House, 1970. [Intellectual history. Paperback.]

133 SOMERVELL, D. C. *English Thought in the Nineteenth Century*. London: Longmans, 1929.

134 STANGE, G. Robert. "The Victorian City and the Frightened Poets." *Victorian Studies*, XI (1968), 627–640.

135 STARKIE, Enid. *From Gautier to Eliot: The Influence of France on English Literature, 1851–1939*. London: Hutchinson, 1960.

136 STARZYK, Lawrence J. " 'That Promised Land': Poetry and Religion in the Early Victorian Period." *Victorian Studies*, XVI (1973), 269–290.

137 STEDMAN, E. C. *Victorian Poets*. Boston: Houghton Mifflin, 1903.

138 STEVENSON, Lionel. "The Pertinacious Victorian Poets." *University of Toronto Quarterly*, XXII (1952), 232–245.

139 SUSSMAN, Herbert L. *Victorians and the Machine: The Literary Response to Technology*. Cambridge: Harvard University Press, 1968. [Includes chapters on Carlyle, Ruskin, Morris, Kipling.]

140 SYMONDSON, Anthony, ed. *The Victorian Crisis of Faith*. London: S.P.C.K., 1970.

141 SYMONS, Arthur. "The Decadent Movement in Literature." *London Quarterly Review*, CXXIX (1918), 89–103.

142 TEMPLEMAN, William D., ed. *Bibliographies of Victorian Literature, 1932–1944*. Urbana: University of Illinois Press, 1945.

143 TINDALL, William York. *Forces in Modern British Literature*. New York: Knopf, 1947. [Also in Vintage Books, V35.]

144 WALKER, Hugh. *The Greater Victorian Poets*, New York: Macmillan, 1895.

145 WALKER, Hugh. *The Literature of the Victorian Era*. Cambridge: Cambridge University Press, 1910.

146 WARREN, Alba H., Jr. *English Poetic Theory, 1825–1865*. Princeton: Princeton University Press, 1950.

147 WATSON, George, ed. *The New Cambridge Bibliography of English Literature*, Vol. III, 1800–1900. Cambridge: Cambridge University Press, 1969.

148 WEINSTEIN, Mark A. *William Edmondstoune Aytoun and the Spasmodic Controversy*. New Haven: Yale University Press, 1968.

149 WEINTRAUB, Stanley, ed. *The Yellow Book: Quintessence of the Nineties*. Garden City, N.Y.: Doubleday, 1964. [Anchor Books, A421.]

150 WELBY, T. Earle. *The Victorian Romantics*. London: Howe, 1929.

151 WELLEK, René. *A History of Modern Criticism, 1750–1950*, Vol. IV: *The Later Nineteenth Century*. New Haven: Yale University Press, 1965.

GENERAL STUDIES

152 WILLEY, Basil. *More Nineteenth Century Studies.* New York: Columbia University Press, 1955.*

153 WILLEY, Basil. *Nineteenth Century Studies.* New York: Columbia University Press, 1950.*

154 WILLIAMS, Raymond. *Culture and Society, 1780–1950.* New York: Columbia University Press, 1958.*

155 WRIGHT, Austin, ed. *Victorian Literature: Modern Essays in Criticism.* New York: Oxford University Press, 1961. [Galaxy Books.]*

156 WRIGHT, Austin, ed. *Bibliographies of Victorian Literature, 1945–1954.* Urbana: University of Illinois Press, 1956.

Anthologies of Victorian Poetry and Prose

157 BECKSON, Karl E., ed. *Aesthetes and Decadents of the 1890's: an Anthology of British Poetry and Prose.* New York: Vintage Books, 1966. [Paperback.]

158 BOWYER, John W., and John L. BROOKS, eds. *The Victorian Age: Prose, Poetry, and Drama.* New York: Appleton-Century-Crofts, 1954.

159 BROWN, E. K. and J. O. BAILEY, eds. *Victorian Poetry.* New York: Ronald Press, 1962.

160 BUCKLER, William E., ed. *Prose of the Victorian Period.* Boston: Houghton Mifflin, 1958. [Riverside Editions, B30.]

161 BUCKLEY, Jerome H., and George B. WOODS, eds. *Poetry of the Victorian Period.* Chicago: Scott-Foresman, 1965.

162 BUCKLEY, Jerome H., ed. *The Pre-Raphaelites.* New York: Modern Library, 1968.

163 CARR, Arthur J., ed. *Victorian Poetry: Clough to Kipling.* New York: Rinehart, 1959. [Rinehart Editions, 96.]

164 HARROLD, Charles F., and William D. TEMPLEMAN, eds. *English Prose of the Victorian Era,* New York: Oxford University Press, 1938.

165 HAYWARD, John, ed. *The Oxford Book of Nineteenth-Century English Verse.* New York: Oxford University Press, 1964.

166 HOFFMAN, Daniel G., and Samuel HYNES, eds. *English Literary Criticism, Romantic and Victorian.* New York: Appleton-Century-Crofts, 1963. [Goldentree Books.]

167 HOUGHTON, Walter E., and G. Robert STANGE, eds. *Victorian Poetry and Poetics.* Boston: Houghton Mifflin, 1968.

168 JOHNSON, E. D. H., ed. *The World of the Victorians.* New York: Scribner, 1964.

169 LANG, Cecil, ed. *The Pre-Raphaelites and Their Circle.* Boston: Houghton Mifflin, 1968. [Riverside Editions B110.]

170 MARTIN, Robert Bernard, ed. *Victorian Poetry: Ten Major Poets.* New York: Random House, 1964.

172 PETERS, Robert L., ed. *Victorians on Art and Literature.* New York: Appleton-Century-Crofts, 1961. [Goldentree Books.]

173 ROE, Frederick W., ed. *Victorian Prose,* New York: Ronald Press, 1947.

174 STEPHENS, James, E. L. BECK, and R. H. SNOW, eds. *Victorian and Later English Poets.* New York: American Book Co., 1937.

175 WILEY, Paul L., and Harold OREL, eds. *British Poetry, 1880–1920.* New York: Appleton-Century-Crofts, 1969.

Individual Poets and Prose Writers

Arnold, Matthew
(1822–1888)

Editions

176 *Works*, 15 vols. London: Macmillan, 1903–1904. [Includes Arnold's letters, edited by G. W. E. Russell, and an extensive bibliography.]

177 TINKER, C. B., and H. F. LOWRY, eds. *The Poetical Works*. New York: Oxford University Press, 1950.

178 ALLOTT, Kenneth, ed. *The Poems of Matthew Arnold*. London: Longmans, 1965.*

179 SUPER, R. H., ed. *Complete Prose Works*. 10 vols. through 1974. Ann Arbor: University of Michigan Press, 1960+ (in progress).*

180 NEIMAN, Fraser, ed. *Essays, Letters and Reviews*. Cambridge: Harvard University Press, 1960.

181 LOWRY, H. F., ed. *Letters of Matthew Arnold to Arthur Hugh Clough*. New York: Oxford University Press, 1932.*

182 LOWRY, H. F., K. YOUNG, and W. H. DUNN, eds. *Note-Books*. Oxford University Press, 1952.

183 ANNAN, Noel, ed. *Selected Essays*. London: Oxford University Press, 1964. [World's Classics.]

184 BROWN, E. K., ed. *Selected Poems. Arlington Heights, Ill.: AHM Publishing Corp., 1951.* [Crofts Classics.]

185 BUCKLER, William E., ed. *Passages from the Prose Writings of Matthew Arnold, Selected by the Author*. New York: New York University Press, 1963.

186 CULLER, A. Dwight, ed. *Poetry and Criticism*. Boston: Houghton Mifflin, 1961. [Riverside Editions, B-55.]

187 MULHAUSER, Frederick L., ed. *Selected Poetry and Prose*. New York: Rinehart, 1953. [Rinehart Editions 62.]

188 TRILLING, Lionel, ed. *The Portable Matthew Arnold*. New York: Viking, 1949.

189 HOCTOR, Sister Thomas Marion, ed. *Essays in Criticism, First Series*. Chicago: University of Chicago Press, 1968.

190 KEATING, P. J., ed. *Matthew Arnold: Selected Prose*. London: Penguin, 1971.

191 SMITH, Peter, and Geoffrey SUMMERFIELD, eds. *Matthew Arnold and the Education of the New Order*. Cambridge: Cambridge University Press, 1969. [Arnold's writings on education.]

Biography

192 BONNEROT, Louis. *Matthew Arnold, poète: Essai de biographie psychologique*. Paris: Didier, 1947.*

193 CHAMBERS, E. K. *Matthew Arnold*. London: Oxford University Press, 1947.

194 JUMP, J. D. *Matthew Arnold*. London: Longmans, 1955.

195 KNICKERBOCKER, W. S. "Matthew Arnold at Oxford." *Sewanee Review*, XXXV (1927), 399–418.

196 PAUL, H. W. *Matthew Arnold*. London: Macmillan, 1925.

197 RUSSELL, G. W. E. *Matthew Arnold*. New York: Scribner, 1904.

198 TREVOR, Meriol. *The Arnolds: Thomas Arnold and His Family*. New York: Scribner, 1973.

199 WARD, Mary A. (Mrs. Humphry). "The Family at Fox How," *A Writer's Recollections*. New York: Harper, 1918.

200 WHITRIDGE, Arnold. *Dr. Arnold of Rugby*. New York: Holt, 1928.

Criticism

201 ALEXANDER, Edward. *Matthew Arnold and John Stuart Mill*. New York: Columbia University Press, 1965.

202 ALEXANDER, Edward. *Matthew Arnold, John Ruskin, and the Modern Temper*. Columbus: Ohio State University Press, 1973.*

203 ALLOTT, Kenneth. "A Background for 'Empedocles on Etna.' " *Essays and Studies*, XXI (1968), 80–100.

204 ALLOTT, Kenneth, *et al*. "The Dating of 'Dover Beach.' " *Notes and Queries*, XIV (1967), 374–376.

205 ALLOTT, Kenneth. *Matthew Arnold*. London: Longmans, 1955.

206 ANDERSON, Warren D. *Matthew Arnold and the Classical Tradition*. Ann Arbor: University of Michigan Press, 1965.

207 BATE, Walter Jackson. "Matthew Arnold." See **155**.

208 BAUM, Paull F. *Ten Studies in the Poetry of Matthew Arnold*. Durham, N.C.: Duke University Press, 1958.

209 BICKLEY, Francis L. *Matthew Arnold and His Poetry*. New York: Dodge, 1911.

210 BRICK, Allan. "Equilibrium in the Poetry of Matthew Arnold." *University of Toronto Quarterly*, XXX (1960), 45–56.

211 BROWN, E. K. "The French Reputation of Matthew Arnold." *Studies in English by Members of University College, Toronto*. Malcolm W. Wallace, ed., Toronto: University of Toronto Press, 1931.

212 BROWN, E. K. *Matthew Arnold: A Study in Conflict*. Chicago: University of Chicago Press, 1948.*

213 BROWN, E. K. *Studies in the Text of Matthew Arnold's Prose Works*. Paris: Imp. P. André, 1935.

214 BUCKLER, William E. *Matthew Arnold's Books: Toward a Publishing Diary*. Geneva: Librarie Droz, 1958.

215 BUCKLEY, Vincent. *Poetry and Morality*. London: Chatto and Windus, 1959.

MATTHEW ARNOLD

216 BUSH, Douglas. *Matthew Arnold. New York: Macmillan, 1971.* [A fine introduction to the life and works. Also a Collier Books paperback.]

217 CHRISTENSEN, Merton A. "Thomas Arnold's Debt to German Theologians: A Prelude to Matthew Arnold's *Literature and Dogma*." *Modern Philology*, LV (1957), 14–20.

218 CONNELL, W. F. *The Educational Thought and Influence of Matthew Arnold*. London: Routledge Kegan Paul, 1950.

219 CONNOLLY, T. L. "Matthew Arnold: Critic." *Thought*, IX (1934), 193–205.

220 COULLING, Sidney M.B. "Matthew Arnold's 1853 Preface: Its Origin and Aftermath." *Victorian Studies*, VII (1964), 233–263.

221 CULLER, A. Dwight. *Imaginative Reason: The Poetry of Matthew Arnold*. New Haven: Yale University Press, 1966.*

222 DAWSON, Carl, ed. *Matthew Arnold: The Poetry: The Critical Heritage*. London: Routledge Kegan Paul, 1973.

223 DE LAURA, David J. "Arnold and Carlyle." *PMLA*, LXXIX (1964), 104–129.

224 DE LAURA, David J. *Hebrew and Hellene in Victorian England: Newman, Arnold, and Pater*. Austin: University of Texas Press, 1969.*

225 DE LAURA, David J. "Matthew Arnold." See **67**.

226 DE LAURA, David J. "Matthew Arnold and the Nightmare of History." See **49**.

227 DE LAURA, David J. "The 'Wordsworth' of Pater and Arnold: 'The Supreme, Artistic View of Life.' " *Studies in English Literature*, VI (1966), 651–667.

228 DEWEY, John. "Matthew Arnold and Robert Browning." John Ratner, ed., *Characters and Events*. New York: Holt, 1929.

229 DONOVAN, Robert A. "The Method of Arnold's Essays in Criticism." *PMLA*, LXXI (1956), 922–931.

230 DREW, Philip. "Matthew Arnold and the Passage of Time: A Study of *The Scholar-Gipsy* and *Thyrsis*." See **39**.

231 DUDLEY, F. A. "Matthew Arnold and Science." *PMLA*, LVII (1942), 275–294.

232 DYSON, A. E. "The Last Enchantments." *Review of English Studies*, VIII (1957), 257–265. [On "The Scholar-Gipsy."]

233 EDGAR, Pelham. "Matthew Arnold as a Writer of Prose." *Dalhousie Review*, I (1921), 247–262.

234 EELLS, J. S. *The Touchstones of Matthew Arnold*. New York: Bookman Associates, 1955.

235 EHRSAM, T. G., *et al. Bibliographies*. See **72**.

236 ELIOT, T. S. "Arnold and Pater," *Selected Essays*. New York: Harcourt Brace, 1932.*

237 FAIRCLOUGH, G. T. *"A Fugitive and Gracious Light": The Relation of Joseph Joubert to Matthew Arnold's Thought*. Lincoln: University of Nebraska Press, 1961.

238 FARRELL, John P. "Homeward Bound: Arnold's Late Criticism." *Victorian Studies*, XVII (1973), 187–206.

239 FARRELL, John P. "Matthew Arnold and the Middle Ages: The Uses of the Past." *Victorian Studies*, XIII (1970), 319–338.

12

MATTHEW ARNOLD

240 FARRELL, John P. "Matthew Arnold's Tragic Vision." *PMIA*, LXXXIV (1970), 107–117.

241 FAVERTY, Frederic E. "Matthew Arnold." See **81**.

242 FAVERTY, Frederic E. *Matthew Arnold, the Ethnologist*. Evanston, Ill.: Northwestern University Press, 1951.

243 FELTES, N. M. "Matthew Arnold and the Modern Spirit." *University of Toronto Quarterly*, XXXII (1962), 27–36.

244 FOERSTER, Norman. "Matthew Arnold and American Letters Today." *Sewanee Review*, XXX (1922), 298–306.

245 FORD, George H. *Keats and the Victorians*. See **83**.

246 FORSYTH, R. A. " 'The Buried Life': The Contrasting Views of Arnold and Clough in the Context of Dr. Arnold's Historiography." *English Literary History*, XXXV (1968), 218–253.

247 FRIEDMAN, Norman. "The Young Arnold, 1847–1849: 'The Strayed Reveller' and 'The Forsaken Merman.' " *Victorian Poetry*, IX (1971), 405–428.

248 FULWEILER, Howard W. *Letters from the Darkling Plain: Language and the Grounds of Knowledge in the Poetry of Arnold and Hopkins*. Columbia: University of Missouri Press, 1972.*

249 FULWEILER, Howard W. "Matthew Arnold: The Metamorphosis of a Merman." *Victorian Poetry*, I (1963), 208–222.

250 GARROD, H. W. *Poetry and the Criticism of Life*. Cambridge: Harvard University Press, 1931.

251 GIANNONE, Richard. "The Quest Motif in 'Thyrsis.' " *Victorian Poetry*, III (1965), 71–80.

252 GOTTFRIED, Leon. *Matthew Arnold and the Romantics*. London: Routledge Kegan Paul, 1963.*

253 GROOM, Bernard. *On the Diction* . . . See **1694**.

254 HANLEY, E. A. *Stoicism in Major English Poets of the Nineteenth Century*. New York: New York University Press, 1948.

255 HARDING, F. J. W. *Matthew Arnold the Critic and France*. Geneva: Librarie Droz, 1964.

256 HARVEY, Charles H. *Matthew Arnold: A Critic of the Victorian Period*. London: Clarke, 1931.

257 HOLLOWAY, John. "Matthew Arnold and the Modern Dilemma." *Essays in Criticism*, I (1951), 1–16.

258 HOUGHTON, Ralph E. *The Influence of the Classics on the Poetry of Matthew Arnold*. Oxford: Blackwell, 1923.

259 HOUGHTON, Walter E. "Arnold's 'Empedocles on Etna.' " *Victorian Studies*, I (1958), 311–336.

260 HUTTON, Richard Holt. "The Poetry of Matthew Arnold," *Literary Essays*. London: Macmillan, 1892.

261 HUTTON Richard Holt. "Two Great Oxford Thinkers: Cardinal Newman and Matthew Arnold," *Essays on Some of the Modern Guides of English Thought in Matters of Faith*. London: Macmillan, 1887.

262 JAMES, D. G. *Matthew Arnold and the Decline of English Romanticism*. London: Oxford University Press, 1961.

263 JAMISON, William A. *Arnold and the Romantics*. Copenhagen: Rosenkilde, Bagger, 1958.

MATTHEW ARNOLD

264 JOHNSON, E. D. H. *The Alien Vision.* See **98**.

265 JOHNSON, Wendell Stacy. *The Voices of Matthew Arnold.* New Haven: Yale University Press, 1961.

266 KELLEHER, John V. "Matthew Arnold and the Celtic Revival." Harry Levin, ed., *Perspectives of Criticism.* Cambridge: Harvard University Press, 1950.

267 KER, W. P. "Matthew Arnold." *The Art of Poetry.* London: Oxford University Press, 1923.

268 KNICKERBOCKER, W. S. "Matthew Arnold's Theory of Poetry." *Sewanee Review*, XXXIII (1925), 440–450.

269 KNIGHT G. Wilson. *"The Scholar-Gipsy:* An Interpretation." *Review of English Studies*, VI (1955), 53–62.

270 KNOEPFLMACHER, U. C. "Dover Revisited: The Wordsworthian Matrix in the Poetry of Matthew Arnold." *Victorian Poetry*, I (1963), 17–26.

271 McCARTHY, Patrick J. *Matthew Arnold and the Three Clases.* New York: Columbia University Press, 1964.*

272 McCARTHY, Patrick J. "Reading Victorian Prose: Arnold's Culture and its Enemies." *University of Toronto Quarterly*, XL (1971), 119–135.

273 MACDONALD, Isobel. *The Buried Self: A Background to the Poems of Matthew Arnold.* London: Davies, 1949.

274 MADDEN, William A. "The Divided Tradition of English Criticism." *PMLA*, LXXIII (1958), 69–80.

275 MADDEN, William A. *Matthew Arnold: A Study of the Aesthetic Temperament in Victorian England.* Bloomington: Indiana University Press, 1967.

276 MIDDLEBROOK, John, ed. *Dover Beach.* Columbus, Ohio: Merrill, 1970. [A casebook.]

277 MURRY, John Middleton. "Matthew Arnold, the Poet," *Discoveries.* London: Collins, 1924.

278 NEIMAN, Fraser. *Matthew Arnold.* New York: Twayne, 1968.

279 NEIMAN, Fraser. "The Zeitgeist of Matthew Arnold." *PMLA*, LXXII (1957), 977–996.

280 PARRISH, Stephen M. *A Concordance to the Poems of Matthew Arnold*, Ithaca, N.Y.: Cornell University Press, 1959.

281 QUILLER-COUCH, Sir Arthur. "Matthew Arnold," *Studies in Literature.* Cambridge: Cambridge University Press, 1920.

282 RALEIGH, John H. *Matthew Arnold and American Culture.* Berkeley: University of California Press, 1957.

283 ROBBINS, William. *The Ethical Idealism of Matthew Arnold.* Toronto: University of Toronto Press, 1959.

284 ROBERTSON, John George. *Matthew Arnold and Goethe.* London: Moring, 1928.

285 ROPER, Alan H. *Arnold's Poetic Landscapes.* Baltimore: Johns Hopkins Press, 1969.

286 SELLS, Iris. *Matthew Arnold and France: The Poet.* New York: Macmillan, 1935.

287 SHERMAN, Stuart P. *Matthew Arnold: How to Know Him.* Indianapolis: Bobbs-Merrill, 1917.

288 SHUMAKER, Wayne. "Matthew Arnold's Humanism: Literature as a Criticism of Life." *Studies in English Literature*, II (1962), 387–402.

289 STANGE, G. Robert. *Matthew Arnold: The Poet as Humanist*. Princeton: Princeton University Press, 1967.

290 STANLEY, Carleton W. *Matthew Arnold*. Toronto: University of Toronto Press, 1938.

291 STEVENSON, Lionel. "Matthew Arnold's Poetry: A Modern Appraisal." *Tennessee Studies in Literature*, IV (1959), 31–41.

292 SUNDELL, M. G. "The Intellectual Background and Structure of Arnold's *Tristram and Iseult*." *Victorian Poetry*, I (1963), 272–283.

293 SUPER, R. H. *The Time-Spirit of Matthew Arnold*. Ann Arbor: University of Michigan Press, 1970.

294 TEMPLE, Ruth Z. *The Critic's Alchemy*. New York: Twayne, 1953. [The first three chapters concern Arnold and French culture.]

295 THORPE, Michael. *Matthew Arnold*. London: Evans, 1969.

296 TILLOTSON, Geoffrey. *Criticism and the Nineteenth Century*. New York: Barnes and Noble, 1952.

297 TILLOTSON, Geoffrey. "Matthew Arnold in Our Time," *Mid-Victorian Studies*. London: Athlone Press, 1965.

298 TILLOTSON, Kathleen. "Matthew Arnold and Carlyle." *Proceedings of the British Academy*, XLII (1956), 133–153.

299 TINKER, C. B., and H. F. LOWRY. *The Poetry of Matthew Arnold*. New York: Oxford University Press, 1940.*

300 TOLLERS, Vincent L., ed. *A Bibliography of Matthew Arnold (1932–1970)*. University Park: Pennsylvania State University Press, 1974.

301 TRILLING, Lionel. *Matthew Arnold*. New York: Columbia University Press, 1949.*

302 VOGELER, Martha Salmon. "Matthew Arnold and Frederic Harrison." *Studies in English Literature*, II (1962), 387–402.

303 WALCOTT, Fred G. *The Origins of Culture and Anarchy*. Toronto: University of Toronto Press, 1970.

304 WATSON, George. "Arnold and the Victorian Mind." *Review of English Literature*, VIII (1967), 33–45.

305 WHITE, Helen C. "Matthew Arnold and Goethe." *PMLA*, XXXVI (1921), 436–453.

306 WILLIAMSON, Eugene L., Jr. *The Liberalism of Thomas Arnold: A Study of His Religious and Political Writings*. University: University of Alabama, 1964.

Browning, Elizabeth Barrett
(1806–1861)

Editions

307 PORTER, Charlotte, and Helen A. CLARKE, eds. *Complete Works*, 6 vols. New York: Crowell, 1900.

308 KENYON, Sir Frederic George, ed. *Poetical Works*. New York: Macmillan, 1897.

309 PRESTON, Harriet W., ed. *Complete Poetical Works*, Cambridge Edition. Boston: Houghton Mifflin, 1900.

310 KENYON, Sir Frederick George, ed. *The Letters of Elizabeth Barrett Browning*. New York: Macmillan, 1899.

311 BROWNING, Robert B., ed. *Letters of Robert Browning and Elizabeth Barrett Browning, 1845–1846*, 2 vols. New York: Harper, 1926.

312 KELLEY, Philip, and Ronald HUDSON, eds. *Diary of E. B. B.* Athens: Ohio University Press, 1969.

313 HEYDON, Peter N., and Philip KELLEY, eds. *Elizabeth Barrett Browning's Letters to Mrs. David Ogilvy, 1849–1861*. New York: Quadrangle, 1973.

314 POPE, Willard B., ed. *Invisible Friends: The Correspondence of Elizabeth Barrett Browning and Benjamin Robert Haydon, 1842–1845*. Cambridge: Harvard University Press, 1972.

Biography

See also Robert Browning

315 BURDETT, Osbert. *The Brownings*. Boston: Houghton Mifflin, 1929.

316 CRESTON, Dormer. *Andromeda in Wimpole Street: The Romance of Elizabeth Barrett Browning*. London: Butterworth, 1929.

317 HEWLETT, Dorothy. *Elizabeth Barrett Browning: A Life*. New York: Knopf, 1952.

318 LUBBOCK, Percy. *Elizabeth Barrett Browning in Her Letters*. London: Smith, 1906.

319 MARKS, Jeannette. *The Family of the Barrett*. New York: Macmillan, 1938.

320 TAPLIN, Gardner B. *The Life of Elizabeth Barrett Browning*. New Haven: Yale University Press, 1957.*

321 WINWAR, Frances. *The Immortal Lovers: Elizabeth Barrett and Robert Browning*. New York: Harper, 1950.

Criticism

322 BALD, Marjory. "Mrs. Browning," *Women Writers of the Nineteenth Century*. Cambridge: Cambridge University Press, 1923.

323 BARBERY, Y. "La Critique moderne face à Elizabeth et Robert Browning." *Études anglaises*, XIII (1960), 444–451.

324 BARNES, Warner. *A Bibliography of Elizabeth Barrett Browning*. Austin: University of Texas Press, 1967.

325 BENSON, Arthur C. "Elizabeth Barrett Browning." *Essays*. New York: Macmillan, 1896.

326 CHESTERTON, G. K. "Elizabeth Barrett Browning." *Varied Types*. New York: Dodd, 1903.

327 EHRSAM, T. G., *et al. Bibliographies*. See **72**.

328 HAYTER, Alethea. *Mrs. Browning*. London: Faber, 1963.*

329 RADLEY, Virginia L. *Elizabeth Barrett Browning*. New York: Twayne, 1972.

330 ROYDS, Kathleen E. *Elizabeth Barrett Browning and Her Poetry*. London: Harrap, 1918.

331 THOMSON, Patricia. "Elizabeth Barrett and George Sand." *Durham University Journal*, XXXIII (1972), 205–219.

332 TIMKO, Michael. "Elizabeth Barrett Browning." See **81**.

333 TOMPKINS J. M. S. *Aurora Leigh*, Fawcell Lecture, 1961–1962. London: Bedford College, 1962.

334 WHITING, Lilian. *A Study of Elizabeth Barrett Browning*. Boston: Little Brown, 1899.

335 WOOLF, Virginia. "Aurora Leigh." *The Second Common Reader*. New York: Harcourt Brace, 1932.

Browning, Robert
(1812–1889)

Editions

336 KENYON, Sir Frederic George, ed. *Works*, 10 vols. London: Smith Elder, 1912.

337 BIRRELL, Augustine, ed. *Complete Poetical Works*. New York: Macmillan, 1915.

338 KING, Roma A., Jr., *et al.*, *The Complete Works of Robert Browning*, 13 vols. Athens: Ohio University Press, 1968+ (in progress).

339 HOOD, Thurman L., ed. *Letters*. New Haven: Yale University Press, 1933.

340 BROWNING, Robert B., ed. *Letters of Robert Browning and Elizabeth Barrett Browning*. See **311**.

341 KINTNER, Elvan, ed. *The Letters of Robert Browning and Elizabeth Barrett Browning*, 2 vols. Cambridge: Harvard University Press, 1970.*

342 STACK, V. E., ed. *How Do I Love Thee?: The Love-Letters of Robert Browning and Elizabeth Barrett*. New York: Putnam, 1969.

343 COLLINS, Thomas J., ed. *The Brownings to the Tennysons: Letters . . . 1852–1889*. Waco, Texas: Armstrong Browning Library, 1971.

344 CURLE, Richard, ed. *Robert Browning and Julia Wedgwood: . . . Letters*. New York: Stokes, 1937.

345 McALEER, Edward C., ed. *Dearest Isa: Robert Browning's Letters to Isabella Blagden*. Austin: University of Texas Press, 1951.

346 DE VANE, William C., and Kenneth L. KNICKERBOCKER, eds. *New Letters*. New Haven: Yale University Press, 1950.

347 HUDSON, Gertrude Reese, ed. *Browning to His American Friends: Letters between the Brownings, the Storys and James Russell Lowell*. Cambridge, England: Bowes, 1965.

348 KNICKERBOCKER, Kenneth L., ed. *Selected Poetry*. New York: Modern Library, 1951. [T-43 MLCE.]

349 SMALLEY, Donald, ed. *Poems*. Boston: Houghton Mifflin, 1956. [Riverside Editions, B3.]

350 SYPHER, Wylie, ed. *The Ring and the Book*. New York: Norton, 1961. [N105-Nort.]

351 ALTICK, Richard D., ed. *The Ring and the Book*. Harmondsworth, England: Penguin, 1971.

Biography

See also Elizabeth Barrett Browning, **315-321**.

352 CHESTERTON, G. K. *Robert Browning*. New York: Macmillan, 1925.

353 CLARKE, Helen A. *Browning and His Century*. New York: Doubleday, 1912.

354 DOWDEN, Edward. *The Life of Robert Browning*. New York: Dutton, 1917.

355 GRIFFIN, W. H. *The Life of Robert Browning*. London: Methuen, 1938.*

356 IRVINE, William, and Park HONAN. *The Book, the Ring, and the Poet*. New York: McGraw-Hill, 1974.*

357 JERMAN, B. R. "The Death of Robert Browning." *University of Toronto Quarterly*, XXXV (1965), 47–74.

358 LOTH, David G. *The Brownings: A Victorian Idyll*. New York: Brentano, 1929.

359 MILLER, Betty. *Robert Browning: A Portrait*. New York: Scribner, 1953.*

360 ORR, Alexandra (Mrs. S.). *The Life and Letters of Robert Browning*, 2 vols. Boston: Houghton Mifflin, 1908.*

361 WARD, Maisie. *Robert Browning and His World*, 2 vols.: Vol. I, *The Private Face, 1812–1861*; Vol. II, *Two Robert Brownings? (1861–1889)*. New York: Holt Rinehart Winston, 1967, 1969.

362 WARD, Maisie. *The Tragi-Comedy of Pen Browning*. London: Sheed and Ward, 1972. [The life of Browning's son.]

Criticism

363 ALTICK, Richard D. " 'A Grammarian's Funeral': Browning's Praise of Folly?" *Studies in English Literature*, III (1963), 449–460.

364 ALTICK, Richard D., and James F. LOUCKS. *Browning's Roman Murder Story: A Reading of the Ring and the Book*. Chicago: University of Chicago Press, 1968.

365 ASSAD, Thomas J. "Browning's 'My Last Duchess.' " *Tulane Studies in English*, X (1961), 117–128.

366 BAKER, Joseph E. "Religious Implications in Browning's Poetry." *Philological Quarterly*, XXXVI (1957), 436–452.

367 BARNES, Warner, ed. *Catalogue of the Browning Collection*. Austin: University of Texas Humanities Research Center, 1966.

368 BERDOE, Edward. *The Browning Cyclopedia: A Guide to the Study of the Works of Robert Browning*. New York: Macmillan, 1950.

ROBERT BROWNING

369 BERMAN, R. J. *Browning's Duke*. New York: Rosen, 1972. [On "My Last Duchess."]

370 BLACKBURN, Thomas. *Robert Browning: A Study of His Poetry*. London: Eyre and Spottiswoode, 1967.

371 BROCKINGTON, A. Allen. *Browning and the Twentieth Century*. New York: Oxford University Press, 1932.

372 BROUGHTON, L. N., and B. F. STELTER. *A Concordance to the Poems of Robert Browning*, 2 vols. New York: Stechert, 1924–1925.

373 BROUGHTON, L. N., C. S. NORTHUP, and Robert PEARSALL, eds. *Robert Browning: A Bibliography, 1830–1950*. Ithaca, N.Y.: Cornell University Press, 1953.

374 CADBURY, William. "Lyric and Anti-Lyric: A Method for Judging Browning." *University of Toronto Quarterly*, XXXIV (1964), 49–67.

375 CAMPBELL, Lily B. *The Grotesque in the Poetry of Robert Browning*. Austin: University of Texas, 1907.

376 CASSIDY, John A. *Study of Browning's "The Ring and the Book."* Boston: Houghton Mifflin, 1924.

377 CHARLTON, H. B. *Browning as Dramatist*. Manchester: John Rylands Library, 1939.

378 CHARLTON, H. B. *Browning as Poet of Religion*. Manchester: Manchester University Press, 1943.

379 CLARKE, Helen A. *Browning's England: A Study of English Influences in Browning*. New York: Baker, 1908.

380 CLARKE, Helen A. *Browning's Italy*. New York: Baker, 1907.

381 COLLINS, Thomas J. "The Poetry of Robert Browning: A Proposal for Reexamination." *Texas Studies in Literature and Language*, XV (1973), 325–340.

382 COLLINS, Thomas J. *Robert Browning's Moral-Aesthetic Theory, 1833–1855*. Lincoln: University of Nebraska Press, 1967.*

383 COOK, A. K. *A Commentary upon Browning's "The Ring and the Book."* London: Oxford University Press, 1920.

384 CORRIGAN, Beatrice. *Curious Annals: New Documents Relating to Browning's Roman Murder Story*. Toronto: University of Toronto Press, 1956.

385 CROWELL, Norton B. *A Reader's Guide to Robert Browning*. Albuquerque: University of New Mexico Press, 1973.

386 CROWELL, Norton B. *The Convex Glass: The Mind of Robert Browning*. Albuquerque: University of New Mexico Press, 1968.*

387 CROWELL, Norton B. *The Triple Soul: Browning's Theory of Knowledge*. Albuquerque: University of New Mexico Press, 1963.

388 CUNDIFF, Paul A. "Andrea del Sarto." *Tennessee Studies in Literature*. XIII (1963), 27–38.

389 CUNDIFF, Paul A. *Browning's Ring Metaphor and Truth*. Metuchen, N.J.: Scarecrow, 1972.

390 CURRY, Samuel Silas. *Browning and the Dramatic Monologue*. Boston: Expression Co., 1908.

391 DE NAGY, N.C. "Pound and Browning." Eva Hesse, ed. *New Approaches to Ezra Pound*. Berkeley: University of California Press, 1969.

392 DE VANE, William C. *A Browning Handbook*. New York: Appleton-Century-Crofts, 1955.*

393 DE VANE, William C. *Browning's Parleyings: The Autobiography of a Mind*. New Haven: Yale University Press, 1927.*

394 DE VANE, William C. "The Landscape of Browning's 'Childe Roland.' " *PMLA*, XL (1925), 426–432.

395 DREW, Philip. "Henry Jones on Browning's Optimism." *Victorian Poetry*, II (1964), 29–41.

396 DREW, Philip. *The Poetry of Robert Browning*. London: Methuen, 1970.*

397 DREW, Philip, ed. *Robert Browning: A Collection of Critical Essays*. Boston: Houghton Mifflin, 1966.

398 DRINKWATER, John. "Browning's Diction." *Victorian Poetry*. New York: Doran, 1924.

399 DUFFIN, Hency C. *Amphibian: A Reconsideration of Browning*. Cambridge, England: Bowes, 1956.

400 DUNCAN, Joseph E. *The Revival of Metaphysical Poetry*. Minneapolis: University of Minnesota Press, 1959. [Contains matter on Browning's debt to Donne.]

401 ELLIOTT, G. R. "The Whitmanism of Browning." *The Cycle of Modern Poetry*. Princeton: Princeton University Press, 1929.

402 FUSON, B. W. *Browning and His English Predecessors in the Dramatic Monolog*. Iowa City: University of Iowa Press, 1948.

403 GLICKSMAN, Harry. "The Legal Aspects of Browning's 'The Ring and the Book.' " *Modern Language Notes*, XXXV (1920), 473–479.

404 GREER, Louise. *Browning and America*. Chapel Hill: University of North Carolina Press, 1952.

405 GRIDLEY, Roy E. *Browning*. London: Routledge Kegan Paul, 1972.

406 GROOM, Bernard. *On the Diction* . . . See **1694**.

407 HAIR, Donald S. *Browning's Experiments with Genre*. Toronto: University of Toronto Press, 1972.

408 HARPER, J. W. " 'Eternity our Due': Time in the Poetry of Robert Browning." See **49**.

409 HARROLD, William E. *The Variance and the Unity: A Study of the Complementary Poems of Robert Browning*. Athens: Ohio University Press, 1973.

410 HATCHER, Harlan H. *The Versification of Robert Browning*. Columbus: Ohio State University Press, 1928.

411 HERMANN, E. A. *The Faith of Robert Browning*. Boston: Sherman, 1916.

412 HONAN, Park. *Browning's Characters: A Study in Technique*. New Haven: Yale University Press, 1961.*

413 HONAN, Park. "Robert Browning." See **81**.

414 HUTTON, Richard Holt. "Robert Browning," *Brief Literary Criticisms*. London: Macmillan, 1906.

415 IRVINE, William. "Four Monologues in Browning's *Men and Women*." *Victorian Poetry*, II (1964), 155–164.

416 JACK, Ian. *Browning's Major Poetry*. London: Oxford University Press, 1973.*

417 JAMES, Henry. "The Novel in *The Ring and the Book*," *Notes on Novelists*. New York: Scribner, 1914.

418 JERMAN, B. R. "Browning's Witless Duke." *PMLA*, LXXII (1957), 488–493. [On "My Last Duchess."]

ROBERT BROWNING

419 JOHNSON, E. D. H. *The Alien Vision*. See **98**.

420 JONES, A. R. "Robert Browning and the Dramatic Monologue: The Impersonal Art." *Critical Quarterly*, IX (1968), 301–328.

421 JONES, Sir Henry. *Browning as a Philosophical and Religious Teacher*. London: Macmillan, 1899.

422 JONES, R. M. *Mysticism in Robert Browning*. New York: Macmillan, 1924.

423 KENMARE, Dallas. *An End to Darkness: A New Approach to Robert Browning and His Work*. London: Owen, 1962.

424 KING, Roma A., Jr. *The Bow and the Lyre: The Art of Robert Browning*. Ann Arbor: University of Michigan Press, 1957.*

425 KING, Roma A., Jr. *The Focusing Artifice: The Poetry of Robert Browning*. Athens: Ohio University Press, 1969.

426 KING, Roma A., Jr., ed. *The Ring and the Book* (Centennial essays). *Victorian Poetry*, VI (1968), 215–375.

427 KNICKERBOCKER, Kenneth L. "A Tentative Apology for Browning." *University of Tennessee Studies in the Humanities*, I (1956), 75–82.

428 KORG, Jacob. "A Reading of *Pippa Passes*." *Victorian Poetry*, VI (1968), 5–19.

429 LANGBAUM, Robert. *The Poetry of Experience: The Dramatic Monologue in Modern Literary Tradition*. New York: Random House, 1957.*

430 LITZINGER, Boyd, and Kenneth KNICKERBOCKER, eds. *The Browning Critics*. Lexington: University of Kentucky Press, 1965.

431 LITZINGER, Boyd, and Donald SMALLEY, eds. *Browning: The Critical Heritage*. London: Routledge Kegan Paul, 1970.

432 LITZINGER, Boyd. *Time's Revenges: Browning's Reputation as a Thinker, 1889–1962*. Knoxville: University of Tennessee Press, 1964.*

433 McALEER, E. C. "Browning's 'Cleon' and Auguste Comte." *Comparative Literature*, VII (1956), 142–145.

434 McCORMACK, James P. "Robert Browning and the Experimental Drama." *PMLA*, LXVIII (1953), 982–991.

435 MARTIN, Hugh. *The Faith of Robert Browning*. London: Student Christian Movement Press, 1963.

436 MAYNE, Ethel C. *Browning's Heroines*. London: Chatto and Windus, 1913.

437 MELCHIORI, Barbara. *Browning's Poetry of Reticence*. New York: Barnes and Noble, 1968.*

438 MIYOSHI, Masao. "Mill and 'Pauline': The Myth and Some Facts." *Victorian Studies*, IX (1965), 154–163.

439 MORE, Paul Elmer. "Why Is Browning Popular?" *Shelburne Essays*, Third Series. New York: Putnam, 1905.

440 ORR, Alexandra (Mrs. S.). *A Handbook to the Works of Robert Browning*. London: Bell, 1902.

441 PETERSON, William E. *Interrogating the Oracle: A History of the London Browning Society*. Athens: Ohio University Press, 1970.

442 PHELPS, W. L. *Robert Browning*. Indianapolis, Ind.: Bobbs-Merrill, 1932.

443 PORTER, Katherine H. *Through a Glass Darkly: Spiritualism in the Browning Circle*. Lawrence: University of Kansas Press, 1958.

444 POSTON, Lawrence, III. "Browning's Poetical Skepticism: *Sordello* and the Plays." *PMLA*, LXXXVIII (1973), 260–270.

21

ROBERT BROWNING

445 POSTON, Lawrence. "Ritual in 'The Bishop Orders his Tomb.'" *Victorian Newsletter*, #17 (1960), 27–28.

446 POSTON, Lawrence, III. "Ruskin and Browning's Artists." *English Miscellany*, XV (1964), 195–212.

447 PREYER, Robert O. "Robert Browning: A Reading of the Early Narratives." *English Literary History*, XXVI (1959), 531–548.

448 PREYER, Robert O. "Two Styles in the Verse of Robert Browning." *ELH*, XXXII (1965), 62–84.

449 PRIESTLEY, F. E. L. "Blougram's Apologetics." *University of Toronto Quarterly*, XV (1946), 139–147.

450 PRIESTLEY, F. E. L. "The Ironic Pattern of Browning's *Paracelsus*." *University of Toronto Quarterly*, XXXIV (1964), 68–81.

451 RAYMOND, William O. *The Infinite Moment, and Other Essays in Robert Browning.* Toronto: University of Toronto Press, 1950.*

452 RIDENOUR, George M. "Browning's Music Poems: Fancy and Fact." *PMLA*, LXXVIII (1963), 369–377.

453 RUSSELL, Frances T. *One Word More on Browning.* Stanford, Cal.: Stanford University Press, 1927.

454 RYALS, Clyde de L. "*Balaustion's Adventure: Browning's Greek Fable.*" *PMLA*, LXXXVIII (1973), 1040–1048.

455 SANDERS, Charles R. "Carlyle, Browning . . ." See **537**.

456 SANTAYANA, George. "The Poetry of Barbarism," *Interpretations of Poetry and Religion.* New York: Scribner, 1900.

457 SESSIONS, Ina Beth. "The Dramatic Monologue." *PMLA*, XLII (1947), 503–516.

458 SHAW, W. David. "Character and Philosophy in 'Fra Lippo Lippi.'" *Victorian Poetry*, II (1964), 127–132.

459 SHAW, W. David. *The Dialectical Temper: The Rhetorical Art of Robert Browning.* Ithaca: Cornell University Press, 1968.

460 SMITH, Charles W. *Browning's Star-Imagery.* Princeton: Princeton University Press, 1941.

461 SOMERVELL, D. C. "The Reputation of Robert Browning." *Essays and Studies*, XV (1929), 122–138.

462 STARKMAN, Miriam. "The Manichee in the Cloister: A Reading of Browning's 'Soliloquy of the Spanish Cloister.'" *Modern Language Notes*, LXXV (1960), 399–405.

463 STEMPEL, Daniel. "Browning's *Sordello:* The Art of the Makers-See." *PMLA*, LXXX (1965), 554-561.

464 SULLIVAN, Mary Rose. *Browning's Voices in "The Ring and the Book."* Toronto: University of Toronto Press, 1969.

465 SYMONS, Arthur. *An Introduction to the Study of Browning.* London: Dent, 1906.

466 THOMPSON, Gordon W. "Authorial Detachment and Imagery in *The Ring and the Book.*" *Studies in English Literature*, X (1970), 669-686.

467 TILLOTSON, Geoffrey. "A Word for Browning." *Sewanee Review*, LXXII (1964), 389-397.

468 TIMKO, Michael. "Browning upon Butler: or, Natural Theology in the English Isle." *Criticism*, VII (1965), 141–150. [On "Caliban" and Browning's own religious position.]

469 TRACY, Clarence, ed. *Browning's Mind and Art*. New York: Barnes and Noble, 1970.

470 WHITLA, William. *The Central Truth: The Incarnation in Browning's Poetry*. Toronto: University of Toronto Press, 1964.

471 WILLOUGHBY, John W. "Browning's 'Childe Roland to the Dark Tower Came.' " *Victorian Poetry*, I (1963), 291–299.

Carlyle, Thomas
(1795–1881)

Editions

472 TRAILL, H. D., ed. *Works*, Centenary Edition, 30 vols. New York: Scribner, 1896–1901.

473 CARLYLE, Alexander, ed. *Letters of Thomas Carlyle to John Stuart Mill, John Sterling, and Robert Browning*. New York: Stokes, 1923.

474 CARLYLE, Alexander, ed. *Love Letters of Thomas Carlyle and Jane Welsh*, 2 vols. London: Lane, 1909.

475 CARLYLE, Alexander, ed. *New Letters of Thomas Carlyle*, 2 vols. London: Lane, 1904.

476 NORTON, Charles Eliot, ed. *Early Letters of Thomas Carlyle, 1814–1826*, 2 vols. London: Macmillan, 1886.

477 NORTON, Charles Eliot, ed. *Letters of Thomas Carlyle, 1826–1836*, 2 vols. London: Macmillan, 1888.

478 NORTON, Charles Eliot, ed. *Correspondence between Goethe and Carlyle*. London: Macmillan, 1887.

479 NORTON, Charles Eliot, ed. *Reminiscences by Thomas Carlyle*, 2 vols. London: Macmillan, 1887. [Reissue in Everyman's Library, 1932.]

480 SLATER, Joseph, ed. *The Correspondence of Emerson and Carlyle*. New York: Columbia University Press, 1964.

481 SANDERS, Charles R., *et al.*, eds. *The Collected Letters of Thomas and Jane Welsh Carlyle*, about 40 vols. projected. Durham, N.C.: Duke University Press, 1970+ (in progress).*

482 MARRS, Edwin W., Jr., ed. *The Letters of Thomas Carlyle to his Brother Alexander with Related Family Letters*. Cambridge: Harvard University Press, 1968.

483 SYMONS, Julian, ed. *Carlyle: Selected Works, Reminiscences, and Letters.* London: Hart-Davis, 1957.

484 TREVELYAN, G. M., ed. *Carlyle: An Anthology*. London: Longmans, 1953.

485 TENNYSON, G. B., ed. *A Carlyle Reader: Selections*. New York: Random House, 1968.

486 SUSSMAN, Herbert, ed. *Sartor Resartus and Selected Prose*. New York: Holt Rinehart Winston, 1970. [Rinehart Editions 144.]

487 CLIVE, John, ed. *History of Friedrich II of Prussia*. Chicago: University of Chicago Press, 1969. [Phoenix Book 344.]

Biography

488 COLLIS, John Stewart. *The Carlyles: A Biography of Thomas and Jane Carlyle*. New York: Dodd Mead, 1972.

489 DUFFY, Sir Charles Gavan. *Conversations with Carlyle*. New York: Scribner, 1892.

490 DUNN, Waldo H. *Froude and Carlyle*. London: Longmans, 1930.

491 FROUDE, James Anthony. *Thomas Carlyle: A History of the First Forty Years of His Life, 1795–1835*, 2 vols. London: Longmans, 1882.*

492 FROUDÉ, James Anthony. *Thomas Carlyle: A History of His Life in London, 1834–1881*, 2 vols. London: Longmans, 1884.*

493 HANSON, L. and E. M. HANSON. *Necessary Evil: The Life of Jane Welsh Carlyle*. New York: Macmillan, 1952.

494 HOLME, Thea. *The Carlyles at Home*. London: Oxford University Press, 1965.

495 ORIGO, Iris. *A Measure of Love*. London: Cape, 1957.

496 ROLLINS, Hyder E. "Charles Eliot Norton and Froude." *Journal of English and Germanic Philology*, LVII (1958), 651–664. [On Carlyle biography.]

497 SCUDDER, Townsendm *Jane Welsh Carlyle*. New York: Macmillan, 1939.

498 SYMONS, Julian. *Thomas Carlyle: The Life and Ideas of a Prophet*. London: Gollancz, 1952.*

499 WILSON, David Alec. *The Life of Thomas Carlyle*, 6 vols. New York: Dutton, 1923–1934.

Criticism

500 BAUMGARTEN, Murray. "Carlyle and 'Spiritual Optics.' " *Victorian Studies*, XI (1968), 503–522.

501 BRANTLINGER, Patrick. " 'Teufelsdröckh' Resartus." *English Language Notes*, IX (1972), 191–193.

502 BROOKES, Gerry H. *The Rhetorical Form of Carlyle's "Sartor Resartus."* Berkeley: University of California Press, 1972.*

503 CABAU, Jacques. *Thomas Carlyle, ou le Promethée enchaîné, 1795–1834*. Paris: Presses Universitaires, 1968.

504 CALDER, G. J. *The Writing of Past and Present*. New Haven: Yale University Press, 1949.*

505 CASSIRER, Ernst. *The Myth of the State*. New Haven: Yale University Press, 1946.

506 CAZAMIAN, Louis. *Carlyle*. New York: Macmillan, 1932.

507 DEEN, Leonard W. "Irrational Form in *Sartor Resartus*." *Texas Studies in Literature and Language*, V (1963), 438–451.

508 DE LAURA, David J. "Arnold and Carlyle." See **223**.

509 DE LAURA, David J. "Ishmael as Prophet: Heroes and Hero-Worship as the Self-expressive Basis of Carlyle's Art." *Texas Studies in Literature and Language*, XI (1969), 705–732.

510 DILTHEY, Wilhelm. *"Sartor Resartus:* Philosophical Conflict, Positive and Negative Eras, and Personal Resolution," 1891 essay translated from the German by Murray Baumgarten and Evelyn Kanes. *Clio*, I (1972), 40–60.

511 DONOVAN, Robert A. "Carlyle and the Climate of Hero-Worship." *University of Toronto Quarterly*, XLII (1973), 122–141.

512 DYER, Isaac W. ed. *A Bibiliography of Carlyle's Writings and Ana.* Portland, Me.: Southworth Press, 1928.

513 GOLDBERG, Michael. *Carlyle and Dickens.* Athens: University of Georgia Press, 1972.

514 GRIERSON, H.J.C. *Thomas Carlyle.* London: Milford, 1941.

515 HARROLD, Charles Frederick. *Carlyle and German Thought, 1819–1834.* New Haven: Yale University Press, 1934.*

516 HOLLOWAY, John. *The Victorian Sage.* See **93**.

517 IKELER, A. Abbott. *Puritan Temper and Transcendental Faith: Carlyle's Literary Vision.* Columbus: Ohio State University Press, 1972.

518 JOHNSON, Wendell Stacy. *Thomas Carlyle: A Study of His Literary Apprenticeship, 1814–1831.* New Haven: Yale University Press, 1911.

519 LA VALLEY, Albert J. *Carlyle and the Idea of the Modern.* New Haven: Yale University Press, 1968.*

520 LEHMAN, B. H. *Carlyle's Theory of the Hero.* Durham, N.C.: Duke University Press, 1928.

521 LEVINE, George. *The Boundaries of Fiction: Carlyle, Macaulay, Newman.* Princeton: Princeton University Press, 1968.

522 LEVINE, George. "The Uses and Abuses of Carlyle." See **103**.

523 MALIN, James C. "Carlyle's Philosophy of Clothes and Swedenborg's." *Scandinavian Studies*, XXXIII (1961), 155–168.

524 MOORE, Carlisle. "Carlyle." C. W. Houtchens and L. H. Houtchens, eds. *The English Romantic Poets and Essayists.* New York: New York University Press, 1966. [A guide to research and scholarship.]

525 MOORE, Carlisle. "The Persistence of Carlyle's 'Everlasting Yea.' " *Modern Philology*, LIV (1957), 187–196.

526 MOORE, Carlisle. " *Sartor Resartus* and the Problem of Carlyle's Conversion." *PMLA*, LXX (1955), 662–681.

527 MUIRHEAD, J. H. "Carlyle's Transcendental Symbolism." *The Platonic Tradition in Anglo-Saxon Philosophy.* London: Macmillan, 1931.

528 NEFF, Emery E. *Carlyle.* New York: Norton, 1932.* [The best short critique of the life and work.]

529 NEFF, Emergy E. *Carlyle and Mill: Mystic and Utilitarian.* New York: Columbia University Press, 1924.

530 ODDIE, William. *Dickens and Carlyle.* London: Centenary Press, 1972.

531 RALLI, A. *A Guide to Carlyle*, 2 vols. London: Allen, 1920.

532 REED, Walter J. "The Pattern of Conversion in *Sartor Resartus.*" *English Literary History*, XXXVIII (1971), 411–431.

533 ROE, Frederick W. *Carlyle as a Critic of Literature.* New York: Columbia University Press, 1910.

534 ROE, Frederick W. *The Social Philosophy of Carlyle and Ruskin.* New York: Smith, 1921.

535 ROELLINGER, Francis X., Jr. "The Early Development of Carlyle's Style." *PMLA*, LXXII (1957), 936–951.

536 ROSENBERG, PHILIP. *The Seventh Hero: Thomas Carlyle and the Theory of Radical Activism.* Cambridge: Harvard University Press, 1974.*

537 SANDERS, Charles R. "Carlyle, Browning, and the Nature of a Poet." *Emory University Quarterly*, XVI (1960), 197–209.

538 SANDERS, Charles R. "Carlyle's Letters to Ruskin." *Bulletin of the John Rylands Library,* XLI (1958), 208–238.

539 SANDERS, Charles R. "The Victorian Rembrandt: Carlyle's Portraits of His Contemporaries." *Bulletin of the John Rylands Library,* XXXIX (1957), 521–527.

540 SEIGEL, Jules Paul, ed. *Thomas Carlyle: The Critical Heritage.* London: Routledge Kegan Paul, 1971.

541 SHARROCK, Roger. "Carlyle and the Sense of History." *Essays and Studies of the English Association,* XIX (1966), 74–91.

542 SHINE, Hill. *Carlyle and the Saint-Simonians.* Baltimore: Johns Hopkins Press, 1941.

543 SHINE, Hill. *Carlyle's Early Reading to 1834.* Lexington: University of Kentucky Libraries, 1953.

544 SHINE, Hill. *Carlyle's Fusion of Poetry, History, and Religion by 1834.* Chapel Hill: University of North Carolina Press, 1938.

545 SMITH, Logan P. "Thomas Carlyle: The Rembrandt of English Prose." See **155**.

546 TAYLOR, A. C. *Carlyle et la Pensée latine.* Paris: Boivin, 1937. [Carlyle's influence on the Continent.]

547 TENNYSON, G. B. *Carlyle and the Modern World.* Edinburgh: Carlyle Society, 1971.

548 TENNYSON, G. B. "Carlyle's Poetry to 1840." *Victorian Poetry,* I (1963), 161–181.

549 TENNYSON, G. B. *Sartor Called Resartus: The Genesis, Structure and Style of Thomas Carlyle's First Major Work.* Princeton: Princeton University Press, 1966.*

550 TENNYSON, G. B. "Thomas Carlyle." See **67**.

551 WORKMAN, Gillian. "Thomas Carlyle and the Governor Eyre Controversy." *Victorian Studies,* XVIII (1974), 77–102.

552 YOUNG, L. M. *Thomas Carlyle and the Art of History.* Philadelphia: University of Pennsylvania Press, 1939.

"Carroll, Lewis" (Dodgson, Charles Lutwidge, 1832–1898)

Editions

553 *The Complete Works of Lewis Carroll.* New York: Modern Library, 1938.

554 GREEN, Roger Lancelyn, ed. *The Diaries of Lewis Carroll.* New York: Oxford University Press, 1954.

555 GREGORY, Horace, ed. *Alice's Adventures in Wonderland, and Through the Looking Glass.* New York: New American Library, 1960. [Signet Books, CD22.]

556 GRAY, Donald J., ed. *Alice in Wonderland*. New York: Norton, 1972. [Text of the *Alice* books and "The Hunting of the Snark" and biographical and critical essays: Norton Critical Edition.]

557 GREEN, Roger Lancelyn, ed. *Alice's Adventures in Wonderland and Through the Looking Glass*. London: Oxford University Press, 1971.

Biography and Criticism

558 AUERBACH, Nina. "Alice and Wonderland: A Curious Child." *Victorian Studies*, XVII (1973), 31–47.

559 AYRES, H. M. *Carroll's Alice*. New York: Columbia University Press, 1936.

560 BLAKE, Kathleen. *Plays, Games, and Sport: The Literary Works of Lewis Carroll*. Ithaca, N.Y.: Cornell University Press, 1974.

561 BOWMAN, Isa. *Lewis Carroll as I Knew Him*. New York: Dover, 1972. [First printed in 1899.]

562 COHEN, Morton, and Roger Lancelyn GREEN. "The Search for Lewis Carroll Letters." *Manuscripts*, XX (1968), 2–15.

563 COLLINGWOOD, S. D. *The Life and Letters of Lewis Carroll*. London: Nelson, 1912.

564 D'AMBROSIO, Michael A. "Alice for Adolescents." *English Journal*, LIX (1970), 1074–1075, 1085.

565 DE LA MARE, W. J. *Lewis Carroll*. London: Faber, 1932.

566 GAFFNEY, Wilbur G. "Humpty Dumpty and Heresy; or, The Case of the Curate's Egg." *Western Humanities Review*, XXII (1968), 131–142.

567 GARDNER, Martin. *The Annotated Alice*. New York: Potter, 1960.*

568 GARDNER, Martin. *The Annotated Snark*. New York: Simon and Schuster, 1962.

569 GREEN, Roger Lancelyn. "Alice's Rail-Journey." *Notes and Queries*, XVI (1969), 217–218.

570 GREEN, Roger Lancelyn. *Lewis Carroll*. London: Bodley Head, 1960.

571 GREEN, Roger Lancelyn. *The Story of Lewis Carroll*. New York: Schuman, 1950.*

572 HUBBELL, G. S. "The Sanity of Wonderland." *Sewanee Review*, XXXV (1927), 387–398.

573 HUDSON, Derek. *Lewis Carroll*. London: Longmans, 1958.

574 HUDSON, Derek. "Lewis Carroll and G. M. Hopkins: Clergymen on a Victorian See-Saw." *Dalhousie Review*, L (1970), 83–87.

575 JOHNSON, Paula. "Alice among the Analysts." *Hartford Studies in Literature*, IV (1972), 114–122.

576 KINCAID, James R. "Alice's Invasion of Wonderland." *PMLA*, LXXXVIII (1973), 92–99.

577 LEACH, Elsie. *"Alice in Wonderland* in Perspective." *Victorian Newsletter*, #25 (1964), 9–11.

578 LENNON, Florence B. *Victoria through the Looking Glass: The Life of Lewis Carroll*. New York: Simon and Schuster, 1945.

579 LEVIN, Harry. "Wonderland Revisited." *Kenyon Review*, XXVII (1965), 591–616.

580 MATTHEWS, Charles. "Satire in the Alice Books." *Criticism*, XII (1971), 105–119.

581 PHILLIPS, Robert, ed. *Aspects of Alice: Lewis Carroll's Dreamchild as Seen Through the Critics' Looking-Glass, 1865–1971*. New York: Vanguard, 1971.

582 RACKIN, Donald. "Alice's Journey to the End of Night." *PMLA*, LXXXI (1966), 313–326.

583 SUTHERLAND, Robert D. *Language and Lewis Carroll*. The Hague: Mouton, 1970.

584 TAYLOR, A. L *White Knight: A Study of C. L. Dodgson (Lewis Carroll)*. Edinburgh: Oliver and Boyd, 1952.*

585 THODY, Philip. "Lewis Carroll and the Surrealists." *Twentieth Century*, CLXIII (1958), 427–434.

586 WALTERS, Jennifer R. "The Disquieting Worlds of Lewis Carroll and Boris Vian." *Revue de Littérature Comparée*. XLVI (1972), 284–294.

587 WEAVER, Warren. *Alice in Many Tongues: The Translations of Alice in Wonderland*. Madison: University of Wisconsin Press, 1964.

588 WILLIAMS, S. H. *A Bibliography of the Writings of Lewis Carroll*. New York: Bowker, 1924.

589 WILLIAMS, S. H., and F. MADAN, *The Lewis Carroll Handbook*. New York: Oxford University Press, 1962.

Clough, Arthur Hugh (1819–1861)

Editions

590 CLOUGH, Mrs. A. H., ed. *Poems and Prose Remains,* 2 vols. London: Macmillan, 1869.

591 NORRINGTON, A. L. P., ed. *The Poems of Arthur Hugh Clough*. London: Oxford University Press, 1968.*

592 LOWRY, Howard F., and Ralph L. RUSK, eds. *Emerson-Clough Letters*. New York: Archon Books, 1968. [Reprint of 1934 edition.]

593 MULHAUSER, Frederick L., ed. *Correspondence*, 2 vols. New York: Oxford University Press, 1957.*

594 TRAWICK, Buckner B., ed. *Selected Prose Works*. University: University of Alabama Press, 1964.

Biography

595 CHORLEY, Lady Katharine. *Arthur Hugh Clough: The Uncommitted Mind*. Oxford: Clarendon Press, 1962.*

596 LEVY, Goldie. *Arthur Hugh Clough*. London: Sidgwick, 1938.

597 LOWRY, Howard F. *Letters of Arnold to Clough*. See **181**.

598 OSBORNE, James L. *Arthur Hugh Clough*. London: Constable, 1920.

599 WILLIAMS, David. *Too Quick Despairer: The Life and Work of Arthur Hugh Clough*. London: Hart-Davis, 1969.*

600 WOODWARD, Frances J. *The Doctor's Disciples: A Study of Four Pupils of Thomas Arnold of Rugby*. London: Oxford University Press, 1954.*

Criticism

601 BAGEHOT, Walter. "Clough's Poems." *Literary Studies*, 3 vols. London: Longmans, 1892.

602 BISWAS, Robindra K. *Arthur Hugh Clough: Towards a Reconsideration*. New York: Oxford University Press, 1972.

603 BROOKE, Stopford A. *Four Victorian Poets*. New York: Putnam, 1908.

604 DE LAURA, David J. "Arnold, Clough, Dr. Arnold, and 'Thyrsis.' " *Victorian Poetry*, VII (1969), 191–202.

605 EHRSAM, T. G. *et al. Bibliographies*. See **72**.

606 FORSYTH, R. A. " 'The Buried Life': Arnold, Clough, and Dr. Arnold." See **246**.

607 GOLLIN, Richard, Walter E. HOUGHTON, and Michael TIMKO, eds. "Arthur Hugh Clough: A Descriptive Catalogue." *Bulletin of New York Public Library*, LXX (1966), 554–585; LXXI (1967), 55–58, 71–92, 173–199.

608 GREENBERGER, Evelyn Barish. *Arthur Hugh Clough: The Growth of a Poet's Mind*. Cambridge: Harvard University Press, 1970.*

609 HARDY, Barbara. "Clough's Self-Consciousness." See **39**.

610 HARRIS, Wendell V. *Arthur Hugh Clough*. New York: Twayne, 1970.*

611 HOUGHTON, Walter E. *The Poetry of Clough*. New Haven: Yale University Press, 1963.*

612 HUTTON, Richard Holt. "Arthur Hugh Clough." *Literary Essays*. London: Macmillan, 1892.

613 LUCAS, F. L. *Eight Victorian Poets*. Cambridge: Cambridge University Press, 1930.

614 McGHEE, Richard D. " 'Blank Misgivings': Arthur Hugh Clough's Search for Poetic Form." *Victorian Poetry*, VII (1969), 105–115.

615 RYALS, Clyde de L. "An Interpretation of Clough's *Dipsychus*." *Victorian Poetry*, I (1963), 182–188.

616 SIDGWICK, Henry. "The Poems and Prose Remains of Arthur Hugh Clough," *Miscellaneous Essays and Addresses*. London: Macmillan, 1904.

617 THORPE, Michael, ed. *Clough: The Critical Heritage*. London: Routledge Kegan Paul, 1972.

618 TIMKO, Michael. "Arthur Hugh Clough." See **81**.

619 TIMKO, Michael. *Innocent Victorian: The Satiric Poetry of Arthur Hugh Clough*. Athens: Ohio University Press, 1966.*

620 TIMKO, Michael. "The Poetic Theory of Arthur Hugh Clough." *English Studies*, XLIII (1962), 240–247.

621 TIMKO, Michael. "The Satiric Poetry of Arthur Hugh Clough." *Victorian Poetry*, I (1963), 104–114.

622 TIMKO, Michael. "The 'True Creed' of Arthur Hugh Clough." *Modern Language Quarterly*, XXI (1960), 208–222.

623 WADDINGTON, Samuel. *Arthur Hugh Clough*. London: Bell, 1883.

624 WOLFE, Humbert. "Arthur Hugh Clough," *The Eighteen-Sixties*, ed. by John Drinkwater. New York: Macmillan, 1932.

Darwin, Charles
(1809–1882)

Editions

625 *The Origin of Species and The Descent of Man*. New York: Modern Library, 1948.

626 PECKHAM, Morse, ed. *The Origin of Species: A Variorum Text*. Philadelphia: University of Pennsylvania Press, 1959.

627 BARLOW, Nora, ed. *Autobiography*. London: Collins, 1958.*

628 BARLOW, Nora, ed. *Diary of the Voyage of H. M. S. "Beagle."* New York: Macmillan, 1933.

629 BARLOW, Nora, ed. *Charles Darwin and the Voyage of the Beagle*. New York: Philosophical Library, 1946. [Unpublished letters and notebooks.]

630 APPLEMAN, Philip, ed. *Darwin*. New York: Norton, 1970. [Selections from Darwin, background materials, modern critical essays.]

631 BARLOW, Nora, ed. *Darwin and Henslow*. Berkeley: University of California Press, 1967. [Letters.]

Biography and Criticism

632 BARNETT, Samuel A., ed. *A Century of Darwin*. London: Heinemann, 1958.

633 BARZUN, Jacques. *Darwin, Marx, Wagner: Critique of a Heritage*. Boston: Little Brown, 1941.

634 CAMPBELL, John A. "Nature, Religion and Emotional Response: A Reconsideration of Darwin's Affective Decline." *Victorian Studies*, XVIII (1974), 159–174.

635 CANNON, Walter F. "Darwin's Vision in *On the Origin of Species*." Max F. Schulz, *et al.*, *Essays in American and English Literature Presented to Bruce Robert McEldberry, Jr.* Athens: Ohio University Press, 1968.

636 DARWIN, Francis. *The Life and Letters of Charles Darwin*, 2 vols. New York: Appleton, 1911.

637 DE BEER, Sir Gavin. *Charles Darwin: Evolution by Natural Selection*. London: Nelson, 1963. [Reissued by Anchor Books, N-41.]*

638 EISELEY, Loren. *Darwin's Century: Evolution and Men who Discovered It*. Garden City: Doubleday, 1958. [A244 Anchor.]*

639 FLEMING, Donald. "Charles Darwin, the Anaesthetic Man." *Victorian Studies*, IV (1961), 219–236.

640 GALE, Barry G. "Darwin and the Concept of a Struggle for Existence: A Study in the Extrascientific Origins of Scientific Ideas." *Isis*, LXIII (1972), 321–344.

CHARLES DARWIN

641 GHISELIN, Michael TM *The Triumph of the Darwinian Method*. Berkeley: University of California Press, 1969.*

642 GLASS, Hiram B., *et al*., eds. *Forerunners of Darwin, 1745–1859*. Baltimore: Johns Hopkins Press, 1959.

643 HALLIDAY, R. J. "Social Darwinism: a Definition." *Victorian Studies*, XIV (1971), 389–405.

644 HIMMELFARB, Gertrude. *Darwin and the Darwinian Revolution*. New York: Doubleday, 1959. [A325 Anchor.]*

645 HOPKINS, Robert S. *Darwin's South America*. New York: Day, 1969.

646 HULL, David L. *Darwin and His Critics: The Reception of Darwin's Theory of Evolution by the Scientific Community*. Cambridge: Harvard University Press, 1973.

647 HUNTLEY, William B. "David Hume and Charles Darwin." *Journal of the History of Ideas*, XXXIII (1972), 457–470.

648 HUXLEY, Thomas Henry. *Darwiniana: Essays*. New York: Appleton, n.d.

649 HYMAN, Stanley E. *The Tangled Bank: Darwin, Marx, Frazer and Freud as Imaginative Writers*. New York: Atheneum, 1962.

650 IRVINE, William. *Apes, Angels, and Victorians*. New York: McGraw-Hill, 1955.*

651 IRVINE, William. "The Influence of Darwin on Literature." *Proceedings of American Philosophical Society*, CIII (1959), 616–628.

652 LOEWENBERG, Bert James. "The Mosaic of Darwinian Thought." *Victorian Studies*, III (1959), 3–18.

653 MacBETH, Norman. *Darwin Retried: An Appeal to Reason*. Boston: Gambit, 1972.

654 MANDELBAUM, Maurice. "Darwin's Religious Views." *Journal of the History of Ideas*, XIX (1958), 363–378.

655 MARSHALL, A. J. *Darwin and Huxley in Australia*. London: Hodder and Stoughton, 1971.

656 MOORE, Ruth E. *Charles Darwin*. New York: Knopf, 1955.

657 MOOREHEAD, Alan. *Darwin and the Beagle*. New York: Harper, 1969.

658 ONG, Walter J., ed. *Darwin's Vision and Christian Perspectives*. New York: Macmillan, 1960.

659 ROGERS, James A. "Darwinism and Social Darwinism." *Journal of the History of Ideas*, XXXIII (1972), 265–280.

660 SEARS, Paul B. *Charles Darwin: The Naturalist as a Cultural Force*. New York: Scribner, 1950.

661 SMITH, Charles K. "Logical and Persuasive Structures in Charles Darwin's Prose Style." *Language and Speech*, III (1970), 243–273.

662 STEVENSON, Lionel. *Darwin among the Poets*. Chicago: University of Chicago Press, 1932.*

663 TAX, Sol, ed. *Evolution after Darwin*, 3 vols. Chicago: University of Chicago Press, 1960.

664 VORZIMMER, Peter J. *Charles Darwin: The Years of Controversy: The "Origin of Species" and its Critics*. Philadelphia: Temple University Press, 1970.

665 WARD, C. H. *Charles Darwin and the Theory of Evolution*. New York: New Home Library, 1943.

666 WELLS, G. H. *Charles Darwin.* London: Routledge, 1937.

667 WHICHLER, Gerhard. *Charles Darwin.* London: Pergamon Press, 1961.

668 WILLEY, Basil. *Darwin and Butler: Two Versions of Evolution.* London: Chatto and Windus, 1960.

669 WOODFIELD, Andrew. "Darwin, Teleology and Taxonomy." *Philosophy*, XLVIII (1973), 35–49.

Dowson, Ernest
(1867–1900)

Editions

670 FLOWER, Desmond, ed. *Poetical Works of Ernest Dowson.* London: Cassell, 1967.

671 LONGAKER, Mark, ed. *The Stories of Ernest Dowson.* Philadelphia: University of Pennsylvania Press, 1947.

672 FLOWER, Desmond, and Henry MAAS, eds. *The Letters of Ernest Dowson.* London: Cassell, 1967.

Biography and Criticism

673 BAKER, Houston A., Jr. "A Decadent's Nature: The Poetry of Ernest Dowson." *Victorian Poetry*, VI (1968), 21–28.

674 DAKIN, Laurence. *Ernest Dowson, the Swan of Lee.* New York: Papyrus Books, 1972.

675 DUFFY, John J. "Ernest Dowson and the Failure of Decadence." *University Review*, XXXIV (1967), 45–49.

676 FOWLER, Rowena. "Ernest Dowson and the Classics." *Yearbook of English Studies*, III (1973), 243–252.

677 GOLDFARB, Russell M. "The Dowson Legend Today." *Studies in English Literature*, IV (1964), 653–662.

678 GOLDFARB, Russell M. "Ernest Dowson Reconsidered." *Tennessee Studies in Literature*, XIV (1970), 61–73.

679 GORDON, Jan B. "Poetic Pilgrimage of Dowson." *Renascence*, XX (1967), 3–10.

680 LONGAKER, Mark. *Ernest Dowson,* 2nd edition. Philadelphia: University of Pennsylvania Press, 1967.*

681 NETZER, A. M. "The Poetry of Ernest Dowson." *Texas Review*, V (1920), 204–208.

682 PLARR, Victor. *Ernest Dowson, 1888–1897: Reminiscences, Unpublished Letters and Marginalia.* New York: Gomme, 1914.

683 REED, John R. "Bedlamite and Pierrot: Ernest Dowson's Esthetic of Futility." *English Literary History*, XXXV (1968), 94–113.

684 SWANN, Thomas B. *Ernest Dowson.* New York: Twayne, 1964.

685 THOMAS, W. R. "Ernest Dowson at Oxford." *Nineteenth Century,* CIII (1928), 560–566.

686 YEATS, William Butler. *Autobiography*. New York: Macmillan, 1953.*

Fitz Gerald, Edward (1809–1883)

Editions

687 BENTHAM, George, ed. *Variorum and Definitive Edition of the Poetical and Prose Writings*, 7 vols. New York: Doubleday, 1902–1903.

688 RICHARDSON, Joanna, ed. *FitzGerald: Selected Works*. London: Hart-Davis, 1962.

689 WEBER, Carl J., ed. *FitzGerald's Rubáiyát*, Centennial Edition. Waterville, Me.: Colby College Press, 1959.

690 HAIGHT, Gordon S.n ed. *The Rubáiyá*. New York: Black, 1942.

691 BUCKLEY, Jerome H., ed. *The Rubáiyát of Omar Khayyám*. New York: Collier Books, 1962. [Collier HS 10.]

692 WRIGHT, W. A., ed. *Letters and Literary Remains*, 7 vols. London: Macmillan, 1903.

693 COHEN, J. M., ed. *Letters*. London: Centaur Press, 1960.

Biography and Criticism

694 ARBERRY, Arthur J. *The Romance of the Rubáiyát*. New York: Macmillan, 1959.

695 BAGLEY, F. R. "Omar Khayyám and FitzGerald." *Durham University Journal*, XXVIII (1967), 81–93.

696 BENSON, Arthur C. *Edward FitzGerald*. New York: Macmillan, 1925.

697 BOYLE, John Andrew. "Omar Khayyám: Astronomer, Mathematician, and Poet." *Bulletin of John Rylands Library*, LII (1969), 30–45.

698 BURGESS, Anthony. "Graves and Omar." *Encounter*, XXX (1968), 77–80.

699 CADBURY, William. "FitzGerald's *Rubáiyát* as a Poem." *ELH*, XXXIV (1967), 541–563.

700 DRAPER, John W. "FitzGerald's Persian Local Color." *West Virginia University Philological Papers*, XIV (1963), 26–56.

701 GRAVES, Robert, and Omar ALI-SHAH. *The Original Rubáiyát of Omar Khayyám*. New York: Doubleday, 1967.

702 HEARN, Lafcadio. "Edward FitzGerald and the *Rubáiyát*," *Interpretations of Literature*, 2 vols. New York: Dodd, 1915.

703 HERON-ALLEN, Edward. *Edward Fitzgerald's Rubáiyát of Omar Khayyám and their Original Persian Sources*. London: Quaritch, 1899.

704 HUTTON, Richard Holt. "A Great Poet of Denial and Revolt," *Brief Literary Criticisms*. London: Macmillan, 1906.

705 PARRINDER, E. G. "Omar Khayyám: Cynic or Mystic?" *London Quarterly and Holborn Review*, CLXXXVII (1962), 222–226.

706 RALLI, A "Edward FitzGerald and His Times," *Critiques*. London: Long-mans, 1927.

707 SHOJAI, Donald A. "The Structure of FitzGerald's Rubáiyát of Omar Khayyám." *Papers of the Michigan Academy of Science, Arts, and Letters*, LII (1967), 369–382.

708 SONSTROEM, David. "Abandon the Day: FitzGerald's *Rubáiyát*." *Victorian Newsletter*, #36 (Fall, 1969), 10–13.

709 TERHUNE, A. M. *The Life of Edward FitzGerald*. New Haven: Yale University Press, 1947.*

710 TIMKO, Michael. "Edward FitzGerald." See **81**.

711 TUTIN, J. R. *A Concordance to FitzGerald's Translation of the Rubáiyát*. London: Macmillan, 1900.

712 WEBER, Carl J. "The 'Discovery' of FitzGerald's Rubáiyát." *Library Chronicle of the University of Texas*, VII (1963), 3–11.

713 WRIGHT, Thomas. *The Life of Edward FitzGerald*, 2 vols. New York: Scribner, 1904.

714 YOHANNAN, John D. "The Fin de Siècle Cult of FitzGerald's 'Rubáiyát.' " *Review of National Literatures*, II (1971), 74–91.

Gilbert, Sir William Schwenck (1836–1911)

Editions

715 *Bab Ballads and Songs of a Savoyard*. London: Macmillan, 1924.

716 *The Bab Ballads*. New York: Macmillan, 1952.

717 *The Savoy Operas*. London: Macmillan, 1953.

718 *The Savoy Operas*, 2 vols. London: Oxford University Press, 1962, 1963. [World's Classics.]

719 *The Complete Plays of Gilbert and Sullivan*. New York: Modern Library, 1936.

720 COLE, WIlliam, ed. *Poems of W. S. Gilbert*. New York: Crowell, 1967.

721 ELLIS, James, ed. *The Bab Ballads*. Cambridge: Harvard University Press, 1971.*

722 ELLIS, James, ed. "The Unsung W. S. Gilbert." *Harvard Library Bulletin*, XVIII (1970), 109–140. [56 uncollected Bab Ballads.]

723 STEDMAN, Jane W., ed. *Gilbert Before Sullivan: Six Comic Plays*. Chicago: University of Chicago Press, 1967.

Biography and Criticism

724 ALLEN, Reginald. "William Schwenck Gilbert: An Anniversary Survey." *Theatre Notebook*, XV (1961), 118–128.

725 AYRE, Leslie. *The Gilbert and Sullivan Companion*. New York: Dodd Mead, 1972.

SIR WILLIAM SCHWENCK GILBERT

726 BAILEY, Leslie. *The Gilbert and Sullivan Book*. New York: Coward McCann, 1957.

727 DARK, Sidney, and R. GREY. *W. S. Gilbert: His Life and Letters*. London: Methuen, 1924.

728 DARLINGTON, W. A. *The World of Gilbert and Sullivan*. New York: Crowell, 1950.

729 DUNHILL, T. F. *Sullivan's Comic Operas*. London: Arnold, 1928.

730 DUNN, G. E. *The Gilbert and Sullivan Dictionary*. New York: Oxford University Press, 1936.

731 GODWIN, A. H. *Gilbert and Sullivan: A Critical Appreciation of the Savoy Operas*. London: Dent, 1926.

732 GOLDBERG, Isaac. *The Story of Gilbert and Sullivan*. New York: Simon, 1928.

733 HALL, Robert A., Jr. "The Satire of *The Yeomen of the Guard*." *Modern Language Notes*, LXXIII (1958), 492–497.

734 HELYAR, James, ed. *Gilbert and Sullivan*. Lawrence: University of Kansas Press, 1972. [Papers from a 1970 G-S conference.]

735 HENSHAW, N. W. "Gilbert and Sullivan Through a Glass Brightly." *Texas Quarterly*, XVI (1973), 48–65.

736 JACOBS, A. *Gilbert and Sullivan*. London: Parrish, 1952.

737 JONES, John Bush. "Gilbert and Sullivan's Serious Satire: More Fact than Fancy." *Western Humanities Review*, XXI (1967), 211–224.

738 JONES, John Bush. "Gilbertian Humor: Pulling Together a Definition." *Victorian Newsletter,* #33 (Spring, 1968), 28–31.

739 JONES, John Bush, ed. *W. S. Gilbert: A Century of Scholarship and Commentary*. New York: New York University Press, 1970.*

740 JONES, John Bush. "W. S. Gilbert's Contributions to Fun, 1865–1874." *Bulletin of New York Public Library*, LXXIII (1969), 253–266.

741 LAWRENCE, Elwood P. " 'The Happy Land': W. S. Gilbert as Political Satirist." *Victorian Studies,* XV (1971), 161–183.

742 MANDER, Raymond, and Joe MITCHENSON. *A Picture History of Gilbert and Sullivan*. London: Vista, 1962.

743 MOORE, Frank L., ed. *The Handbook of Gilbert and Sullivan*. New York: Crowell, 1972.

744 PEARSON, Hesketh. *Gilbert and Sullivan*. New York: Harper, 1935.

745 PEARSON, Hesketh. *Gilbert: His Life and Strife*. London: Methuen, 1957.*

746 PURDY, C. L. S. *Gilbert and Sullivan*. New York: Messner, 1947.

747 QUILLER-COUCH, Sir Arthur: "W. S. Gilbert," *Studies in Literature*, 3 vols. New York: Putnam, 1918.

748 REVITT, Paul J. "Gilbert and Sullivan: More Seriousness than Satire." *Western Humanities Review*, XIX (1965), 19–34.

749 STEDMAN, Jane W. "The Genesis of Patience." *Modern Philology*, LXVI (1968), 48–58.

750 WILLIAMSON, A. *Gilbert and Sullivan Opera: A New Assessment*. New York: Macmillan, 1953.

Hardy, Thomas
(1840–1928)

Editions

751 *Works*, Wessex Edition, 37 vols. London: Macmillan, 1912–1914.

752 *Collected Poems*. New York: Macmillan, 1953.

753 RANSOM, John Crowe, ed. *Selected Poems*. New York: Macmillan, 1961. [MP 57.]

754 WEBER, Carl J., ed. *Hardy's Love Poems*. New York: Macmillan, 1963.

755 YOUNG, G. M., ed. *Selected Poems*. New York: Macmillan, 1940.

756 *The Dynasts*. London: Macmillan, 1927.

757 HARDY, Evelyn, and F. B. PINION, eds. *One Rare Fair Woman: Thomas Hardy's Letters to Florence Henniker, 1893–1922*. London: Macmillan, 1972.

758 OREL, Harold, ed. *Thomas Hardy's Personal Writings*. Lawrence: University Press of Kansas, 1969. [Also Kansas Paperback.]

Biography

759 BLUNDEN, Edmund. *Thomas Hardy*. New York: Macmillan, 1952.

760 DEACON, Lois, and Terry COLEMAN. *Providence and Mr. Hardy*. London: Hutchinson, 1966. [Contentious data and speculation on Hardy's early life.]

761 HARDY, Evelyn. *Thomas Hardy*. New York: St. Martin's Press, 1954.*

762 HARDY, Evelyn, and Robert GITTINGS, eds. *Some Recollections by Emma Hardy and Some Relevant Poems by Thomas Hardy*. London: Oxford University Press, 1961.

763 HARDY, Florence E. *The Life of Thomas Hardy, 1840–1928*. London: Macmillan, 1962.*

764 HOGAN, Don. "Biography and Mr. Hardy." *Victorian Studies,* XI (1967), 98–102.

765 KAY-ROBINSON, Denys. *Hardy's Wessex Reappraised*. New York: St. Martin's Press, 1972.

766 STEWART, J. I. M. *Thomas Hardy: A Critical Biography*. New York: Dodd Mead, 1971.

767 WEBER, Carl J. *Hardy of Wessex: His Life and Literary Career*. New York: Columbia University Press, 1940.* Revised ed., 1965.

Criticism

768 BAILEY, J. O. "Evolutionary Meliorism in the Poetry of Thomas Hardy." *Studies in Philology*, LX (1963), 569–587.

769 BAILEY, J. O. *The Poetry of Thomas Hardy: A Handbook and Commentary*. Chapel Hill: University of North Carolina Press, 1970.*

THOMAS HARDY

770 BAILEY, J. O. *Thomas Hardy and the Cosmic Mind: A New Reading of The Dynasts*. Chapel Hill: University of North Carolina Press, 1956.

771 BEACH, Joseph Warren. *The Technique of Thomas Hardy*. Chicago: University of Chicago Press, 1922.

772 BRENNECKE, Ernest. *Thomas Hardy's Universe*. New York: Columbia University Press, 1926.

773 BROOKS, Jean R. *Thomas Hardy: The Poetic Structure*. Ithaca: Cornell University Press, 1971.*

774 CHAKRAVARTY, Amiya. *"The Dynasts" and the Post-War Age in Poetry*. New York: Oxford University Press, 1938.

775 CHEW, Samuel C. *Thomas Hardy, Poet and Novelist*. New York: Knopf, 1928.

776 COX. R. G., ed. *Thomas Hardy: The Critical Heritage*. London: Routledge Kegan Paul, 1970.

777 DAVIE, Donald. *Thomas Hardy and British Poetry*. New York: Oxford University Press, 1972.*

778 DUFFIN, H. C. *Thomas Hardy: A Study of the Wessex Novels, the Poems, and the Dynasts*. New York: Longmans, 1937.

779 ELLIOTT, A. P. *Fatalism in the Works of Thomas Hardy*. Philadelphia: University of Pennsylvania Press, 1935.

780 GERBER, Helmut, and W. Eugene DAVIS, eds. *Thomas Hardy: An Annotated Bibliography of Writings about Him*. De Kalb: Northern Illinois University Press, 1973.

781 GUERARD, Albert J., ed. *Hardy: A Collection of Critical Essays*. Englewood Cliffs, N.J.: Prentice-Hall, 1963.

782 GUERARD, Albert J. *Thomas Hardy*. New York: New Directions, 1964.

783 HAWKINS, Desmond. *Thomas Hardy*. London: Barker, 1951.

784 HICKSON, C. *The Versification of Thomas Hardy*. Philadelphia: University of Pennsylvania Press, 1931.

785 HONE, J. M. "The Poetry of Mr. Hardy." *London Mercury,* V (1922), 396–405.

786 HORNBECK, Bert G. *The Metaphor of Chance: Vision and Technique in the Works of Thomas Hardy*. Athens: Ohio University Press, 1972.

787 HOWE, Irving. "The Short Poems of Thomas Hardy." *Southern Review*, II (1966), 878–905.

788 HOWE, Irving. *Thomas Hardy*. New York: Macmillan, 1967.

789 HYNES, Samuel L. *The Pattern of Hardy's Poetry*. Chapel Hill: University of North Carolina Press, 1961.*

790 JOHNSON, Lionel. *The Art of Thomas Hardy*. New York: Dodd, 1923.

791 JOHNSON, Trevor. *Thomas Hardy*. London: Evans, 1968.

792 KING. R. W. "The Lyrical Poems of Thomas Hardy." *London Mercury*, XV (1926), 157–170.

793 KING. R. W. "Verse and Prose Parallels in the Work of Thomas Hardy." *Review of English Studies,* VIII (1962), 52–61.

794 LOWES, John L. "Two Readings of Earth." *Yale Review,* XV (1926), 515–539.

795 MARSDEN, Kenneth. *The Poems of Thomas Hardy: A Critical Introduction*. New York: Oxford University Press, 1969.*

THOMAS HARDY

796 MAXWELL, D. *The Landscape of Thomas Hardy.* London: Cassell, 1928.

797 MAY, Charles E. "Thomas Hardy and the Poetry of the Absurd." *Texas Studies in Literature and Language*, XII (1970), 63–73.

798 MEISEL, Perry. *Thomas Hardy: The Return of the Repressed.* New Haven: Yale University Press, 1972.

799 MILLER, J. Hillis. "History as Repetition in Thomas Hardy's Poetry." See **49**.

800 MILLER, J. Hillis. *Thomas Hardy: Distance and Desire.* Cambridge: Harvard University Press, 1970.*

801 MORGAN, William W. "Form, Tradition, and Consolation in Hardy's 'Poems of 1912–13.'" *PMLA*, LXXXIX (1974), 496–505.

802 MURRY, John Middleton. "The Poetry of Mr. Hardy," Aspects of Literature. New York: Knopf, 1921.

803 OREL, Harold. *Thomas Hardy's Epic-Drama: A Study of "The Dynasts."* New York: Greenwood Press, 1969.

804 OREL, Harold. "Trends in Critical Views Toward Hardy's Poetry." *English Literature in Transition*, XIV (1971), 223–239.

805 PERKINS, David. "Hardy and the Poetry of Isolation." *English Literary History*, XXVI (1959), 253–270. [Also in Guerard, see **781**.]

806 PINION, F. B. *A Hardy Companion.* London: Macmillan, 1968.

807 PURDY, R. L. *Thomas Hardy: A Bibliographical Study.* New York: Oxford University Press, 1954.*

808 RUTLAND, WILLIAM R. *Thomas Hardy: A Study of His Writings and Their Background.* Oxford: Blackwell, 1938.

809 SAXELBY, F. O. *A Thomas Hardy Dictionary.* London: Routledge, 1911.

810 SIEMENS, Lloyd. "Parody in the Poems of Thomas Hardy." *Dalhousie Review*, LII (1972), 111–128.

811 SMITH, R. M. "Philosophy in Thomas Hardy's Poetry." *North American Review*, CCXX (1924), 330–340.

812 *Southern Review*, Thomas Hardy Centennial Issue, VI (1940), 1–224. [Essays on Hardy by fourteen able critics.]*

813 SOUTHERINGTON, F. R. *Hardy's Vision of Man.* New York: Barnes and Noble, 1971.

814 SOUTHWORTH, J. G. *The Poetry of Thomas Hardy.* New York: Columbia University Press, 1947.

815 STEVENSON, Lionel. "Thomas Hardy." See **81**.*

816 STEWART, J. I. M. *Eight Modern Writers.* New York: Oxford University Press, 1963. [Contains chapters on Hardy and Kipling.]

817 TAYLOR, E. Dennis. "The Riddle of Hardy's Poetry." *Victorian Poetry*, XI (1973), 263–276.

818 VAN DOREN, Mark. "The Poems of Thomas Hardy," *Four Poets on Poetry*, ed. by D. C. Allen. Baltimore: Johns Hopkins Press, 1959.

819 WAIN, John. "The Poetry of Thomas Hardy." *Critical Quarterly*, VIII (1966), 166–173.

820 WEBER, Carl J. *Hardy in America.* Waterville, Maine: Colby College Press, 1946.

821 WEBSTER, Harvey C. *On a Darkling Plain: The Art and Thought of Thomas Hardy.* Chicago: University of Chicago Press, 1947.

822 WEDMORE, F. "Thomas Hardy's Poems," *Certain Comments*. London: Selwyn, 1925.

823 WILLIAMS, Charles. *Poetry at Present*. New York: Oxford University Press, 1930. [Includes discussions of Hardy, Housman, Kipling.]

824 WILLIAMS, Merryn. *Thomas Hardy and Rural England*. New York: Columbia University Press, 1972.

825 WRIGHT, Walter F. *The Shaping of "The Dynasts."* Lincoln: University of Nebraska Press, 1967.

826 ZIETLOW, Paul. *Moments of Vision: The Poetry of Thomas Hardy*. Cambridge: Harvard University Press, 1974.*

Henley, William Ernest (1849–1903)

Editions

827 *Works*, 7 vols. London: Nutt, 1908.

828 *Works,* 5 vols. London: Macmillan, 1921.

829 HALLAM, J. H. "Some Early Letters and Verses of W. E. Henley." *Blackwood's*, CCLIV (1943), 200–209.

830 PARKER, W. M. "W. E. Henley: Twenty-five New Poems: A Centenary Discovery." *Poetry Review*, XL (1949), 188–199.

Biography and Criticism

831 BUCKLEY, Jerome H. *William Ernest Henley: A Study in the Counter-Decadence of the 'Nineties*. Princeton: Princeton University Press, 1945.*

832 COHEN, Edward H. *The Henley-Stevenson Quarrel*. Gainesville: University Presses of Florida, 1974.

833 CONNELL, John. *W. E. Henley*. London: Constable, 1949.*

834 CORNFORD, Leslie Cope. *William Ernest Henley*. London: Constable, 1913.

835 DRINKWATER, John. "William Ernest Henley." *The Muse in Council*. Boston: Houghton Mifflin, 1925.

836 FLORA, Joseph M. *William Ernest Henley*. New York: Twayne, 1970.

837 GREGORY, Horace. "On William Ernest Henley," *The Shield of Achilles*. New York: Harcourt Brace, 1944.

838 HIND, C. Lewis. "W. E. Henley," *Authors and I*. New York: Lane, 1921.

839 LOW, Sidney. "William Ernest Henley: Some Memories and Impressions." *Living Age*, CCXXXIX (1903), 150–158.

840 MARRIOTT-WATSON, H. B. "Living Critics: I, "William Ernest Henley." *Bookman*, II (1895), 186–188.

841 MASTERMAN, C. F. G. "William Ernest Henley," *In Peril of Change*. New York: Huebsch, 1905.

842 NEFF, Marietta. "The Place of Henley." *North American Review,* CCXI (1920), 555–563.

843 NICHOLS, W. B. "The Influence of Henley." *Living Age,* CCCX (1921), 88–92.

844 NIVEN, Frederick. "Henley." *Library Review,* XXVII (1933), 93–98.

845 NOYES, Alfred. "The Poetry of W. E. Henley," *Some Aspects of Modern Poetry.* London: Hodder, 1924.

846 SCHAEFER, William D. "Henley and 'The Hound of Heaven.' " *Victorian Poetry,* V (1967), 171–181.

847 SCHAPPES, Morris U. "William Ernest Henley's Principles of Criticism." *PMLA,* XLVI (1931), 1289–1301.

848 SHIELDS, Roden. "A Blurred Memory of Childhood." *Cornhill,* XIX (1905), 223–228.

849 SQUIRE, J. C. "Henley," *Books Reviewed.* New York: Doran, 1922.

850 STEPHEN, Herbert. "Henley as a Contemporary and an Editor." *London Mercury,* XIII (1926), 387–400.

851 SYMONS, Arthur. "Some Makers of Modern Verse," *Forum,* LXVI (1921), 476–488.

852 WILLIAMSON, Kennedy. *W. E. Henley: A Memoir.* London: Shaylor, 1930.

853 WOODS, Margaret L. "Poets of the Eighties," *The Eighteen Eighties.* See **68**.

Hopkins, Gerard Manley (1844–1889)

Editions

854 BRIDGES, Robert, ed. *Poems of Gerard Manley Hopkins.* London: Oxford University Press, 1918.

855 GARDNER, W. H., and Norman H. MacKENZIE, eds. *The Poems of Gerard Manley Hopkins,* Fourth Edition. New York: Oxford University Press, 1967.

856 GARDNER, W. H., ed. *Selected Poems and Prose.* London: Penguin Books, 1953. [Penguin D15.]

857 PICK, John, ed. *A Hopkins Reader.* New York: Oxford University Press, 1953. [Reissued as Image Book paperback.]

858 HOUSE, Humphry, ed. *The Notebooks and Papers.* New York: Oxford University Press, 1937. [Second edition, 2 vols., completed by Christopher Devlin and Graham Storey, 1959.]

859 ABBOTT, C. C., ed. *The Letters of Gerard Manley Hopkins to Robert Bridges, and The Correspondence of Gerard Manley Hopkins and Richard Watson Dixon,* 2 vols. New York: Oxford University Press, 1955.

860 ABBOTT, C. C., ed. *Further Letters.* New York: Oxford University Press, 1956.

Biography

861 LAHEY, G. F. *The Life of Father Gerard Manley Hopkins*. New York: Oxford University Press, 1938.*

862 PICK, John. *Gerard Manley Hopkins, Priest and Poet*. New York: Oxford University Press, 1942.*

863 RITZ, Jean-Georges. *Robert Bridges and Gerard Hopkins, 1863–1889: A Literary Friendship*. London: Oxford University Press, 1960.*

864 RUGGLES, Eleanor. *Gerard Manley Hopkins*. New York: Norton, 1944.

Criticism

865 BALL, Patricia M. *The Science of Aspects: The Changing Role of Fact in the Work of Coleridge, Ruskin and Hopkins*. New York: Oxford University Press, 1971.*

866 BAUM, Paull F. "Sprung Rhythm." *PMLA*, LXXIV (1959), 418–425.

867 BENDER, Todd K. *Gerard Manley Hopkins: The Classical Background and Critical Reception of His Work*. Baltimore: Johns Hopkins Press, 1966.

868 BOYLE, Robert R. *Metaphor in Hopkins*. Chapel Hill: University of North Carolina Press, 1961.

869 CHARNEY, Maurice. "A Bibliographical Study of Hopkins Criticism, 1918–1940." *Thought*, XXV (1950), 297–326.

870 CHEVIGNY, Bell Gale. " 'Instress' and Devotion in the Poetry of Gerard Manley Hopkins." *Victorian Studies*, IX (1965), 141–153.

871 COHEN, Edward H. ed. "A Comprehensive Hopkins Bibliography: 1863–1918." *Bulletin of Bibliography*, XXV (1967), 79–81.

872 COHEN, Edward H., ed. *Works and Criticism of Gerard Manley Hopkins: A Comprehensive Bibliography*. Washington, D.C.: Catholic University of America Press, 1969.

873 COHEN, S. J. "The Poetic Theory of Gerard Manley Hopkins." *Philological Quarterly*, XXVI (1947), 1–20.

874 COLLINS, Winston. "Tennyson and Hopkins." *University of Toronto Quarterly*, XXXVIII (1968), 84–95.

875 COTTER, James Finn. *Inscape: The Christology and Poetry of Gerard Manley Hopkins*. Pittsburgh: University of Pittsburgh Press, 1972.

876 DILLIGAN, R. J., and Todd K. BENDER. *A Concordance to the English Poetry of Gerard Manley Hopkins*. Madison: University of Wisconsin Press, 1970.

877 DOWNES, David A. *Gerard Manley Hopkins: A Study of His Ignatian Spirit*. New York: Bookman Associates, 1959.

878 DOWNES, David A. *Victorian Portraits: Hopkins and Pater*. New York: Bookman Associates, 1965.

879 EAGLETON, Terry. "Nature and the Fall in Hopkins: A Reading of 'God's Grandeur.' " *Essays in Criticism*, XXIII (1973), 68–75.

880 FULWEILER, Howard W. *Letters from a Darkling Plain*. See **248**.

881 GARDNER, W. H. *Gerard Manley Hopkins, 1844–1889*, 2 vols. New Haven: Yale University Press, 1948–1949.*

GERARD MANLEY HOPKINS

882 GIBSON, Walker, "Sound and Sense in G. M. Hopkins." *Modern Language Notes,* LXXIII (1958), 95–100.

883 HARRISON, T. P. "The Birds of Gerard Manley Hopkins." *Studies in Philology,* LIV (1957), 968–978.

884 HARTMAN, Geoffrey H., ed. *Hopkins: A Collection of Critical Essays.* Englewood Cliffs, N.J.: Prentice-Hall, 1966.

885 HEUSER, Alan. *The Shaping Vision of Gerard Manley Hopkins.* New York: Oxford University Press, 1958.*

886 HOLLOWAY, Sister M. M. *The Prosodic Theory of Gerard Manley Hopkins.* Washington, D.C.: Catholic Univeristy of America Press, 1947.

887 HUNTER, Jim. *Gerard Manley Hopkins.* London: Evans, 1966.

888 HUNTLEY, John F. "Hopkins' 'The Windhover' as a Prayer of Request." *Renascence,* XV (1964), 154–162.

889 JOHNSON, Wendell Stacy. *Gerard Manley Hopkins: The Poet as Victorian.* Ithaca: Cornell University Press, 1968.*

890 KEATING, John E. *The Wreck of the Deutschland: An Essay and a Commentary.* Kent, Ohio: Kent State University Press, 1963.

891 KELLY, Bernard. *The Mind and Poetry of Gerard Manley Hopkins.* Boston: Humphries, 1935.

892 KENYON CRITICS (*Kenyon Review*). *Gerard Manley Hopkins.* Norfolk, Conn.: New Directions, 1946.

893 LEAVIS, F. R. *New Bearings in English Poetry.* New York: Stewart, 1950.

894 LEES, Francis Noel. *Gerard Manley Hopkins.* New York: Columbia University Press, 1966. [Columbia Essays paperback.]

895 McCHESNEY, Donald. *A Hopkins Commentary.* New York: New York University Press, 1968.

896 MacKENZIE, Norman H. *Hopkins.* London: Oliver and Boyd, 1968. [Also paperback.]

897 McNAMARA, Peter L. "Motivation and Meaning in the 'Terrible Sonnets.' " *Renascence,* XVI (1964), 78–80.

898 McNAMEE, M. B. "Mastery and Mercy in *The Wreck of the Deutschland.*" *College English,* XXIII (1962), 267–276.

899 MARIANI, Paul L. *A Commentary on the Complete Poems of Gerard Manley Hopkins.* Ithaca: Cornell University Press, 1971.*

900 MARTIN, Philip M. *Mastery and Mercy: A Study of Two Religious Poems, The Wreck of the Deutschland by G. M. Hopkins and Ash Wednesday by T. S. Eliot.* London: Oxford University Press, 1957.

901 MELLOWN, Elgin W. "The Reception of Gerard Manley Hopkins' Poems, 1918–1930." *Modern Philology,* LXIII (1965), 38–51.

902 MILWARD, Peter. *A Commentary on G. M. Hopkins' "The Wreck of the Deutschland."* London: Hurst, 1968.

903 MONTAG, George E. "The Windhover: Crucifixion and Redemption." *Victorian Poetry,* III (1965), 109–118.

904 MURPHY, Michael W. "Violent Imagery in the Poetry of Gerard Manley Hopkins." *Victorian Poetry,* VII (1969), 1–16.

905 MYERS, John A., Jr. "Intimations of Mortality: An Analysis of Hopkins's 'Spring and Fall.' " *English Journal,* LI (1962), 585–587.

ALFRED EDWARD HOUSMAN

906 PETERS, W. A. M. *Gerard Manley Hopkins: A Critical Study*. New York: Oxford University Press, 1948.*

907 PHARE, Elsie E. *The Poetry of Gerard Manley Hopkins*. New York: Macmillan, 1933.

908 PICK, John. "Gerard Manley Hopkins." See **81**.

909 PICK, John, ed. *Gerard Manley Hopkins: "The Windhover."* Columbus, Ohio: Merrill, 1969. [A casebook.]

910 PREYER, Robert O., " 'The Fine Delight that Fathers Thought.' " See **49**.

911 RAINE, Kathleen. "Hopkins: Nature and Human Nature." *Sewanee Review,* LXXXI (1973), 201–224.

912 SCHNEIDER, Elisabeth W. *The Dragon in the Gate: Studies in the Poetry of G. M. Hopkins*. Berkeley: University of California Press, 1968.*

913 SCHOECK, R. J. "Influence and Originality in Hopkins." *Renascence*, IX (1956), 77–89.

914 STEMPEL, Daniel. "A Reading of 'The Windhover.' " *College English,* XXIII (1962), 305–307.

915 SULLOWAY, Alison G. *Gerard Manley Hopkins and the Victorian Temper*. New York: Columbia University Press, 1972.*

916 SUTHERLAND, John. " 'Tom's Garland': Hopkins' Political Poem." *Victorian Poetry*, X (1972), 111–121.

917 WARREN, Austin. "Instress of Inscape." See **155**.

918 WEYAND, Norman, and R. V. SCHODER, eds. *Immortal Diamond: Studies in Gerard Manley Hopkins*. New York: Sheed, 1949.

919 WOLFE, Patricia. "The Paradox of Self: A Study of Hopkins' Conflict in the 'Terrible Sonnets.' " *Victorian Poetry,* VI (1968), 85–103.

920 WOODRING, Carl R. "Once More 'The Windhover.' " *Western Review,* XV (1950), 61–64.

921 ZABEL, Morton D. "Gerard Manley Hopkins: Poetry as Experiment and Unity." *Poetry,* XXXVII (1930), 152–161.

Housman, Alfred Edward (1859–1936)

Editions

922 *Collected Poems*. New York: Holt, 1940.

923 *The Name and Nature of Poetry*. New York: Macmillan, 1933.

924 CARTER, John, ed. *A. E. Housman: Selected Prose*. Cambridge: Cambridge University Press, 1961.

925 HABER, Tom Burns, ed. *Complete Poems*. New York: Holt Rinehart Winston, 1959.

926 CARTER, John, ed. *The Collected Poems of A. E. Housman*. New York: Holt Rinehart Winston, 1965.

927 MAAS, Henry, ed. *The Letters of A. E. Housman*. Cambridge: Harvard University Press, 1971.

928 DIGGLE, J., and F. R. D. GOODYEAR, eds. *The Classical Papers of A. E. Housman,* 3 vols. London: Cambridge University Press, 1973.

929 WEBER, Carl J., ed. *A Shropshire Lad.* New York: Heritage, 1951.

Biography and Criticism

930 BRONOWSKI, J. *The Poet's Defence.* New York: Macmillan, 1939.

931 EHRSAM, T. G. *A Bibliography of Alfred Edward Housman.* Boston: Faxon, 1941.

932 ELLIS, S. M. "A. E. Housman," *Mainly Victorian.* London: Hutchinson, 1925.

933 GOW, S. F. *A. E. Housman: A Sketch.* New York: Macmillan, 1936.

934 HABER, Tom Burns. "Housman and Lucretius." *Classical Journal,* LVIII (1963), 173–182.

935 HABER, Tom Burns. "Housman's Poetic Method: His Lectures and Notebooks." *PMLA*, LXIX (1954), 1000–1016.

936 HABER, Tom Burns. *The Making of "A Shropshire Lad."* Seattle: University of Washington Press, 1966.*

937 HAMILTON, Robert. *Housman the Poet.* London: Lee, 1953.

938 HAWKINS, Maude. *A. E. Housman, Man Behind a Mask.* Chicago: Regnery, 1958.

939 HOUSMAN, Laurence. *My Brother, A. E. Housman: Personal Recollections Together with Thirty Hitherto Unpublished Poems.* New York: Scribner, 1938.

940 HYDER, C. K., ed. *A Concordance to the Poems of A. E. Housman.* Lawrence: University of Kansas Press, 1940.

941 JARRELL, Randall. "Texts from Housman." *Kenyon Review,* I (1939), 260–271.

942 LEA, Gordon B. "Ironies and Dualities in *A Shropshire Lad." Colby Library Quarterly*, X (1973), 71–79.

943 LEGGETT, B. J. *Housman's Land of Lost Content: A Critical Study of "A Shropshire Lad."* Knoxville: University of Tennessee Press, 1970.*

944 LUCAS, Frank L. *The Greatest Problem.* London: Cassell, 1960.

945 MARLOW, Norman. *A. E. Housman: Scholar and Poet.* Minneapolis: University of Minnesota Press, 1958.

946 REEDY, George, S. J. "Housman's Use of Classical Convention." *Victorian Poetry,* VI (1968), 51–61.

947 RICKS, Christopher, ed. *A. E. Housman.* Englewood Cliffs, N.J.: Prentice Hall, 1968. [Critical essays by various hands.]*

948 ROBINSON, Oliver. *Angry Dust: The Poetry of A. E. Housman.* Boston: Humphries, 1950.

949 SPENDER, Stephen. *The Making of a Poem.* New York: Norton, 1963.

950 STALLMAN, R. W. "Annotated Bibliography of A. E. Housman." *PMLA,* LX (1945), 463–502.

951 STEVENSON, Lionel. "Alfred Edward Housman." See **81.**

952 STOZIER, Robert I. "A. E. Housman: Image, Illogic and Allusion." *Colby Library Quarterly,* VII (1966), 257–263.

953 WATSON, G. L. *A. E. Housman: A Divided Life*. Boston: Beacon Press, 1958.

954 WHITE, William. "A. E. Housman: A Critical and Bibliographical Review of Books about the Poet, 1936–1955." *Journal of English and Germanic Philology*, LVI (1959), 242–250.

955 WILLIAMS, Charles. *Poetry at Present*. See **823**.

956 WILSON, Edmund. "A. E. Housman." *The Triple Thinkers*. New York: Harcourt Brace, 1938.

957 WITHERS, P. *A Buried Life: Personal Recollections of A. E. Housman*. London: Cape, 1940.

Huxley, Thomas Henry
(1825–1895)

Editions

958 *Selected Works of Thomas Henry Huxley,* 9 vols. New York: Appleton, n.d. [Reprints collected essays 1893–1894; the whole Reprinted, 1968.]

959 HUXLEY, Julian, ed. *Diary of the Voyage of H. M. S. Rattlesnake*. Garden City: Doubleday, 1936.

960 FOSTER, Michael, and E. Ray LANKESTER, eds. *Scientific Memoirs*, 5 vols. London: Macmillan, 1898–1903.

961 BIBBY, Cyril, ed. *T. H. Huxley on Education: A Selection from his Writings*. Cambridge: Cambridge University Press, 1973.

962 BIBBY, Cyril, ed. *The Essence of T. H. Huxley: Selections from his Writings*. London: Macmillan, 1967.

Biography and Criticism

963 ASHFORTH, Albert. *Thomas Henry Huxley*. New York: Twayne, 1969.

964 AYRES, C. E. *Huxley*. New York: Norton, 1932.

965 BIBBY, Cyril. *Scientist Extraordinary: The Life and Scientific Works of Thomas Henry Huxley, 1825–1895*. New York: St. Martin's, 1972.*

966 BIBBY, Cyril. *T. H. Huxley: Scientist, Humanist, and Educator*. London: Watts, 1959.

967 BICKNELL, John W. "Thomas Henry Huxley." See **67**.

968 BLINDERMAN, Charles S. "Thomas Henry Huxley." *Scientific Monthly*, LXXXIV (1957), 171–182.

969 BLINDERMAN, Charles S. "T. H. Huxley's Thoery of Aesthetics." *Journal of Aesthetics and Art Criticism*, XXI (1962), 49–55.

970 CLARK, Ronald W. *The Huxleys*. New York: McGraw Hill, 1968.*

971 CLODD, Edward. *Thomas Henry Huxley*. New York: Dodd, 1902.

972 DOCKRILL, D. W. "T. H. Huxley and the Meaning of 'Agnosticism.' " *Theology*, LXXIV (1971), 461–477.

973 EISEN, Sydney. "Huxley and the Positivists." *Victorian Studies*, VII (1964), 336–358.

974 GARDNER, Joseph H. "A Huxley Essay as 'Poem.'" *Victorian Studies*, XIV (1970), 177–191.

975 HOUGHTON, Walter E. "The Rhetoric of T. H. Huxley." *University of Toronto Quarterly*, XVIII (1949), 159–175.

976 HUXLEY, Aldous. "T. H. Huxley as a Man of Letters," *The Olive Tree*. New York: Harper, 1937.

977 HUXLEY, Leonard. *Life and Letters of Thomas Henry Huxley*, 2 vols. New York: Appleton, 1900.*

978 HUXLEY, Leonard. *Thomas Henry Huxley: A Character Sketch*. London: Watts, 1920.

979 IRVINE, William. *Apes, Angels, and Victorians*. See **650**.*

980 IRVINE, William. "Carlyle and T. H. Huxley." See **155**.

981 IRVINE, William. *Thomas Henry Huxley (Writers and their Work)*. London: Longmans, 1960.

982 McBRIDE, F. W. *Huxley*. London: Duckworth, 1934.

983 MARSHALL, A. J. *Darwin and Huxley in Australia*. See **655**.

984 MITCHELL, P. Chalmers. *Huxley: A Sketch of his Life and Work*. New York: Putnam, 1900.

985 NASH, J. V. "A Biological Interpretation of Politics." *Open Court*, XXXVII (1923), 296–306.

986 NOLAND, Richard W. "T. H. Huxley on Culture." *Personalist*, XLV (1964), 94–111.

987 PETERSON, Houston. *Huxley: Prophet of Science*. London: Longmans, 1932.

988 RANDAL, William P. "Huxley in America." *Proceedings of the American Philosophical Society*, CXIV (1970), 73–99.

989 ROSE, Phyllis. "Huxley, Holmes, and the Scientist as Aesthete." *Victorian Newsletter*, #38 (Fall, 1970), 22–24.

Kipling, Rudyard (1865–1936)

Editions

990 *Complete Works*, Sussex Edition, 35 vols. London: Macmillan, 1937.

991 *Collected Works*, Burwash Edition, 28 vols. New York: Doubleday, 1941.

992 *Collected Verse*. New York: Doubleday, 1946.

993 ELIOT, T. S., ed. *A Choice of Kipling's Verse*. New York: Scribner, 1943.

994 CARRINGTON, Charles, ed. *The Complete Barrack-Room Ballads*. London: Methuen, 1973.

Biography

995 BERESFORD, G. C. *Schooldays with Kipling*. New York: Putnam, 1936.

996 CARPENTER, L. R. *Rudyard Kipling: A Friendly Profile*. Chicago: Argus, 1942.

997 CARRINGTON, C. E. *Rudyard Kipling*. New York: Doubleday, 1955.*

998 COHEN, Morton. "Rudyard Kipling and Rider Haggard." *Dalhousie Review*, XL (1960), 297–322.

999 HOPKINS, R. T. *The Kipling Country*. London: Palmer, 1924.

1000 MANSFIELD, M. F. *A Kipling Notebook*. New York: Mansfield, 1899. [Issued also under title *Kiplingiana*.]

1001 RICE, H. C. *Rudyard Kipling in New England*. Brattleboro, Vt.: Book Cellar, 1951.

Criticism

1002 ANNAN, Noel. "Kipling's Place in the History of Ideas." *Victorian Studies*, III (1960), 323–348.

1003 ARCHER, William. *Poets of the Younger Generation*. London: Lane, 1902.

1004 BODELSEN, C. A. *Aspects of Kipling's Art*. Manchester: Manchester University Press, 1963.

1005 BRAYBROOKE, Patrick. *Kipling and His Soldiers*. Philadelphia: Lippincott, 1926.

1006 BROWN, Hilton. *Rudyard Kipling*. New York: Harper, 1945.

1007 BUSHNELL, Nelson S. "Kipling's Ken of India." *University of Toronto Quarterly*, XXVII (1957), 62–78.

1008 CHESTERTON, G. K. *Heretics*. New York: Lane, 1905.

1009 CORNELL, Louis L. *Kipling in India*. New York: St. Martin's Press, 1966.

1010 CROFT-COOKE, R. *Rudyard Kipling*. London: Home, Van Thal, 1948.

1011 DEUTSCH, Karl, and Norbert WIENER. "The Lonely Nationalism of Rudyard Kipling." *Yale Review*, LII (1963), 499–517.

1012 DOBRÉE, Bonamy. *Rudyard Kipling: Realist and Fabulist*. London: Oxford University Press, 1967.

1013 DURAND, R. A. *A Handbook to the Poetry of Rudyard Kipling*. London: Hodder, 1917.

1014 ELIOT, T. S. "Rudyard Kipling." *Mercure de France*, CCXXXV (1959), 5–15.

1015 GILBERT, Elliot L., ed. *Kipling and the Critics*. London: Peter Owen, 1965.

1016 GILMER, H. W. "The Classical Element in the Poems of Rudyard Kipling." *Classical Weekly*, XIV (1921), 178–181.

1017 GREEN, Roger Lancelyn, ed. *Kipling: The Critical Heritage*. London: Routledge Kegan Paul, 1971.

1018 GROSS, John, ed. *Rudyard Kipling: The Man, His Work and His World*. New York: Simon and Shuster, 1972.

1019 HENN, T. R. *Kipling*. London: Oliver and Boyd, 1968.*

1020 KERNAHAM, Coulson. *Six Famous Living Poets*. London: Butterworth, 1922.

1021 LIVINGSTON, Flora V. *Bibliography of the Works of Rudyard Kipling.* New York: Wells, 1927. *Supplement.* Cambridge: Harvard University Press, 1938.

1022 MacMUNN, G. F. *Rudyard Kipling, Craftsman.* Toronto: Ryerson Press, 1938.

1023 RUTHERFORD, Andrew, ed. *Kipling's Mind and Art.* Stanford: Stanford University Press, 1964.

1024 RUTHERFORD, Andrew. *Some Aspects of Kipling's Verse.* London: Oxford University Press, 1967.*

1025 SAXTON, E. F. *The Kipling Index.* New York: Doubleday, 1911.

1026 SHANKS, E. B. *Rudyard Kipling: A Study in Literature and Political Ideas.* New York: Doubleday, 1940.*

1027 STEWART, J. I. M. *Eight Modern Writers.* See **816**.

1028 STEWART, J. I. M. *Rudyard Kipling.* New York: Dodd Mead, 1966.*

1029 STEWART, James. *Rudyard Kipling: A Bibliographical Catalogue.* Toronto: University of Toronto Press, 1959.

1030 TOMPKINS, J. M. S. *The Art of Rudyard Kipling.* London: Methuen. 1959.*

1031 WEYGANDT, A. M. *Kipling's Reading and Its Influence on His Poetry.* Philadelphia: University of Pennsylvania Press, 1939.

1032 WILLIAMS, Charles. *Poetry at Present.* See **823**.

1033 WILSON, Edmund. "The Kipling Nobody Read." *The Wound and the Bow.* Boston: Houghton Mifflin, 1941.

1034 YOUNG, W. Arthur, and John H. McGIVERING. *A Kipling Dictionary.* London: Macmillan, 1968.

Lear, Edward
(1812–1888)

Editions

1035 JACKSON, Holbrook, ed. *The Complete Nonsense of Edward Lear.* New York: Dover, 1951.

1036 MOSS, Howard, ed. *The Nonsense Books of Edward Lear.* New York: New American Library, 1964. [Signet Books, CT243.]

1037 STRACHEY, Lady, ed. *Queery Leary Nonsense.* London: Mills, 1911.

1038 STRACHEY, Lady, ed. *Letters.* London: Unwin, 1907.

1039 STRACHEY, Lady, ed. *Later Letters.* New York: Duffield, 1911.

1040 *Edward Lear in Corsica: The Journal of a Landscape Painter.* London: Kimber, 1966.

Biography and Criticism

1041 CAMMAERTS, E. *The Poetry of Nonsense.* London: Routledge, 1925.

1042 DAVIDSON, Angus. *Edward Lear: Landscape Painter and Nonsense Poet.* London: Murray, 1968.*

1043 HOFER, Philip. *Edward Lear as a Landscape Draughtsman.* Cambridge: Harvard University Press, 1967.

1044 HOFER, Philip. "The Yonghy Bonghy Bo." *Harvard Library Bulletin,* XV (1967), 229–237.*

1045 MALCOLM, I. "The Literary Work of Edward Lear." *Cornhill Magazine,* XCVII (1908), 25–36.

1046 MILLER, Edmund. "Two Approaches to Edward Lear's Nonsense Songs." *Victorian Newsletter,* #44 (Fall, 1973), 5–8.

1047 NOAKES, VIVIEN. *Edward Lear: The Life of a Wanderer.* Boston: Houghton Mifflin, 1969.*

1048 SEWELL, E. *Field of Nonsense.* London: Chatto and Windus, 1952.

Macaulay, Thomas Babington (1800–1859)

Editions

1049 *Works,* 8 vols. New York: Longmans, 1897.

1050 *Complete Writings,* 20 vols. Boston: Houghton Mifflin, 1899–1900.

1051 *Critical and Historical Essays,* 3 vols. Boston: Houghton Mifflin, 1925.

1052 TREVELYAN, G. M., ed. *Lays of Ancient Rome and Other Historical Poems.* London: Longmans, 1928.

1053 YOUNG, G. M., ed. *Macaulay: Prose and Poetry.* Cambridge: Harvard University Press, 1953.

1054 CLIVE, John, and Thomas PINNEY, eds. *Thomas Babington Macaulay: Selected Writings.* Chicago: University of Chicago Press, 1972.

1055 TREVOR-ROPER, Hugh, ed. *Macaulay: Critical and Historical Essays.* London: Macmillan, 1965.

Biography and Criticism

1056 ABBOTT, W. C. "Macaulay and the New History." *Yale Review,* XVIII (1929), 539–557.

1057 BEATTY, R. C. *Lord Macaulay: Victorian Liberal.* Norman: University of Oklahoma Press, 1938.

1058 BRYANT, Arthur. *Macaulay.* New York: Appleton, 1933.

1059 CLIVE, John. "Macaulay's Historical Imagination." *Review of English Literature,* I (1960), 20–28.

1060 CLIVE, John. *Macaulay: The Shaping of the Historian.* New York: Knopf, 1973.*

1061 CLIVE, John, and Thomas PINNEY. "Thomas Babington Macaulay." See **67.**

1062 DAVIES, Godfrey. "The Treatment of Constitutional History in Macaulay's History of England." *Huntington Library Quarterly,* II (1939), 179–204.

1063 FIRTH, Sir Charles. *Commentary on Macaulay's History of England.* London: Macmillan, 1938.

1064 FONG, David. "Macaulay: The Essayist as Historian." *Dalhousie Review,* LI (1971), 38–48.

1065 FRASER, G. S. "Macaulay's Style as an Essayist." *Review of English Literature,* I (1960), 9–19.

1066 GEYL, Pieter. "Macaulay in his Essays," *Debates with Historians.* London: Batsford, 1955.

1067 KNOWLES, David. *Lord Macaulay, 1800–1959.* Cambridge: Cambridge University Press, 1960. [Macaulay and the critics.]

1068 LEVINE, George. "Macaulay: Progress and Retreat," *The Boundaries of Fiction.* Princeton: Princeton University Press, 1968.

1069 MADDEN, William. "Macaulay's Style," *The Art of Victorian Prose.* See **103.**

1070 MILLGATE, Jane. *Macaulay.* London: Routledge Kegan Paul, 1973.*

1071 POTTER, George R. *Macaulay (Writers and Their Work).* London: Longmans, 1959.

1072 ROBERTS, S. C. *Lord Macaulay: The Pre-eminent Victorian.* London: Oxford University Press, 1927.

1073 ROWSE, A. L. "Macaulay's Essays." See **155.**

1074 SIRKIN, Gerald, and Natalie ROBINSON. "The Battle of Indian Education: Macaulay's Opening Salvo." *Victorian Studies,* XIV (1971), 407–428.

1075 THOMSON, Mark A. *Macaulay.* London: Routledge Kegan Paul, 1959.

1076 TREVELYAN, G. O. *The Life and Letters of Lord Macaulay,* 2 vols. London: Oxford University Press, 1923.*

1077 WEBER, Ronald. "Singer and Seer: Macaulay on the Historian as Poet." *Papers on Language and Literature,* III (1967), 210–219.

1078 WILLIAMS, S. T. "Macaulay's Reading and Literary Criticism." *Philological Quarterly,* III (1924), 119–131.

1079 YODER, Edwin M., Jr. "Macaulay Revisited." *South Atlantic Quarterly,* LXIII (1964), 542–551.

Meredith, George (1828–1909)

Editions

1080 *Works,* 36 vols. London: Constable, 1914.

1081 MEREDITH, W. M., ed. *Letters of George Meredith,* 2 vols. New York: Scribner, 1912.

1082 CLINE, C. L., ed. *The Letters of George Meredith,* 3 vols. New York: Oxford University Press, 1970.*

1083 TREVELYAN, G. M., ed. *Poetical Works.* New York: Scribner, 1928.*

1084 LEWIS, C. Day, ed. *Modern Love.* London: Hart-Davis, 1948.

Biography

1085 BUTCHER, Lady. *Memories of George Meredith*. London: Constable, 1919.

1086 ELLIS, S. M. "George Meredith: His Association with the Pre-Raphaelites." *London Bookman*, LXXIII (1928), 253–257.

1087 GALLAND, René. *George Meredith: les cinquante premières années*. Paris: Les Presses françaises, 1923.

1088 GRETTON, Mary. *The Writings and Life of George Meredith*. Cambridge: Harvard University Press, 1926.

1089 HAMMERTON, J. A. *George Meredith: His Life and Art in Anecdote and Criticism*. Edinburgh: Grant, 1911.

1090 LINDSAY, Jack. *George Meredith: His Life and Work*. London: Bodley Head, 1956.

1091 PRIESTLEY, J. B. *George Meredith*. London: Macmillan, 1926.

1092 SASSOON, Siegfried. *Meredith*. New York: Viking, 1948.

1093 STEVENSON, Lionel. *The Ordeal of George Meredith*. New York: Scribner, 1953.*

Criticism

1094 AUSTIN, Deborah. "Meredith on the Nature of Metaphor." *University of Toronto Quarterly*, XXVII (1957), 96–102.

1095 BARTLETT, Phyllis. "George Meredith: Early Manuscript Poems in the Berg Collection." *Bulletin of the New York Public Library*, LXI (1957), 396–415.

1096 BEACH, Joseph Warren. *The Comic Spirit in George Meredith*. New York: Longmans, 1911.

1097 BEACH, Joseph Warren. *The Concept of Nature*. See **45**.

1098 BOGNER, Delmar. "The Sexual Side of Meredith's Poetry." *Victorian Poetry*, VIII (1970), 107–126.

1099 CHAMBERS, E. K. "Meredith's *Modern Love*" and "Meredith's Nature Poetry," *A Sheaf of Studies*. London: Oxford University Press, 1942.

1100 CHESTERTON, G. K. "George Meredith." *The Uses of Diversity*. New York: Dodd, 1921.

1101 CLUTTON-BROCK, Arthur. "George Meredith," *More Essays on Books*. New York: Dutton, 1921.

1102 EDGAR, Pelham. "Poetry of George Meredith." *Living Age*, CCLV (1907), 744–751.

1103 ESDAILE, A. J. K. *A Chronological List of George Meredith's Publications*. London: Constable, 1914.

1104 FORMAN, M. Buxton, ed. *A Bibliography of the Writings in Prose and Verse of George Meredith*. London: Bibliographical Society, 1922.

1105 FORMAN, M. Buxton, ed. *Meredithiana*. London: Bibliographical Society, 1924.

1106 FRIEDMAN, Norman. "The Jangled Harp: Symbolic Structure in *Modern Love*." *Modern Language Quarterly*, XVII (1957), 9–26.

1107 HAIGHT, Gordon S. "George Meredith and the *Westminster Review*." *Modern Language Review*, LIII (1958), 1–16.

1108 HENLEY, William Ernest. "Meredith," *Views and Reviews*. London: Macmillan, 1921.

1109 JACKSON, Holbrook. "The Ideas of George Meredith," *All Manner of Folk*. London: Richards, 1912.

1110 KELVIN, Norman. *A Troubled Eden: Nature and Society in the Works of George Meredith*. Stanford, Cal.: Stanford University Press, 1961.*

1111 MONROE, Harriet, "Meredith as a Poet." *Poetry*, XXXII (1928), 210–216.

1112 PEEL, R. *The Creed of a Victorian Pagan*. Cambridge: Harvard University Press, 1931.

1113 PRITCHETT, V. S. *George Meredith and English Comedy*. New York: Random House, 1969. [Chiefly on the novels.]

1114 REVELL, W. F. "George Meredith's Nature Poetry." *Westminster Review*, CXLII (1894), 506–523.

1115 REYNOLDS, George F. "Two Notes on the Poetry of George Meredith." *University of Colorado Studies*, XV (1925), 1–12.

1116 SAWIN, H. L. "George Meredith: A Bibliography of Meredithiana. 1920–1953." *Bulletin of Bibliography*, XXI (1955), 186–191, 215–216.

1117 SIMPSON, Arthur L., Jr. "Meredith's Pessimistic Humanism: A New Reading of *Modern Love*." *Modern Philology*, LXVII (1970), 341–356.

1118 STEVENSON, Lionel. "George Meredith." See **81**.

1119 TREVELYAN, G. M. *The Poetry and Philosophy of George Meredith*. London: Constable, 1912.*

1120 TUCKER, Cynthia Grant. "Meredith's Broken Laurel: *Modern Love* and the Renaissance Sonnet Tradition." *Victorian Poetry*, X (1972), 351–365.

1121 WILLIAMS, Ioan, ed. *Meredith: The Critical Heritage*. London: Routledge Kegan Paul, 1971.

1122 WOODS, Alice. *George Meredith as Champion of Women and of Progressive Education*. Oxford: Blackwell, 1937.

1123 WRIGHT, Elizabeth Cox. "The Significance of Image Patterns in Meredith's *Modern Love*." *Victorian Newsletter*, #13 (1958), 1–9.

1124 WRIGHT, Walter F. *Art and Substance in George Meredith*. Lincoln: University of Nebraska Press, 1953.*

Mill, John Stuart (1806–1873)

Editions

1125 ROBSON, John M., *et al.*, eds. *The Works of John Stuart Mill*, 25 projected vols. Toronto: University of Toronto Press, 1963+ (in progress).*

1126 COSS, J. J., ed. *Autobiography*. New York: Columbia University Press, 1944.

1127 STILLINGER, Jack, ed. *The Early Draft of John Stuart Mill's Autobiography*. Urbana: University of Illinois Press, 1961.

1128 CASTELL, Alburey, ed. *On Liberty*. Arlington Heights, Ill.: AHM Publishing Corp., 1947. [Crofts Classics.]

1129 LINDSAY, A. D., ed. *Utilitarianism, Liberty, and Representative Government*. New York: Dutton, 1950. [Everyman's Library.]

1130 LEAVIS, F. R., ed. *On Bentham and Coleridge*. New York: Harper, 1964. [Harper Torchbooks, TB1070.]

1131 HAYEK, F. A., ed. *The Spirit of the Age*. Chicago: University of Chicago Press, 1942.

1132 ELLIOT, H. R. S., ed. *The Letters of John Stuart Mill*, 2 vols. London: Longmans, 1910.

1133 ALEXANDER, Edward, ed. *John Stuart Mill: Literary Essays*. Indianapolis: Bobbs-Merrill, 1967. [Paperback.]

1134 LERNER, Max, ed. *Essential Works of John Stuart Mill*. New York: Bantam, 1965. [Bantam Matrix paperback.]

1135 MILL, Anna J., ed. *John Mill's Boyhood Visit to France*. Toronto: University of Toronto Press, 1960. [Journal and notebook.]

Biography and Criticism

1136 ALEXANDER, Edward. *Matthew Arnold and John Stuart Mill*. See **201**.

1137 ALEXANDER, Edward. "Mill's Theory of Culture: The Wedding of Literature and Democracy." *University of Toronto Quarterly*, XXXV (1965), 75–88.

1138 ANSCHUTZ, R. F. *The Philosophy of John Stuart Mill*. London: Oxford University Press, 1953.

1139 AUGUST, Eugene R. "Mill as Sage: The Essay on Bentham." *PMLA*, LXXXIX (1974), 142–153.

1140 AUGUST, Eugene R. "Mill's *Autobiography* as Philosophic *Commedia*." *Victorian Poetry*, XI (1973), 143–162.

1141 BORCHARD, Ruth. *John Stuart Mill the Man*. London: Watts, 1957.

1142 BRITTON, Karl. *John Stuart Mill*. London: Penguin Books, 1953.*

1143 CARR, Robert. "The Religious Thought of John Stuart Mill: A Study in Reluctant Skepticism." *Journal of the History of Ideas*, XXIII (1962), 475–495.

1144 COWLING, Maurice. *Mill and Liberalism*. Cambridge: Cambrige University Press, 1963.

1145 CRANSTON, Maurice. "J. S. Mill as a Political Philosopher." *History Today*, VII (1958), 38–46.

1146 HAMBURGER, Joseph. *Intellectuals in Politics: John Stuart Mill and the Philosophical Radicals*. New Haven: Yale University Press, 1965.*

1147 HARRISON, Frederic. *John Stuart Mill*. New York: Macmillan, 1896.

1148 HAYEK, F. A. *John Stuart Mill and Harriet Taylor: Their Correspondence and Subsequent Marriage*. Chicago: University of Chicago Press, 1951.

1149 HIMMELFARB, Gertrude. *On Liberty and Liberalism: The Case of John Stuart Mill*. New York: Knopf, 1974.*

1150 HOLLOWAY, Harry A. "Mill's *Liberty*, 1859–1959." *Ethics*, LXXI (1961), 130–132.

1151 McCLOSKEY, H. J. *John Stuart Mill: A Critical Study*. London: Macmillan, 1971.*

1152 MacMINN, Ney, *et al.*, eds. *Bibliography of the Published Writings of John Stuart Mill*. Evanston, Ill.: Northwestern University Press, 1970 (first published, 1945).

1153 MILL, Anna J. "John Stuart Mill and the Picturesque." *Victorian Studies,* XIV (1970), 151–163.

1154 MILLETT, Kate. "The Debate over Women: Ruskin versus Mill." *Victorian Studies,* XIV (1970), 63–82.

1155 MORLAN, G. *America's Heritage from John Stuart Mill.* New York: Columbia University Press, 1936.

1156 MORRIS, John N. *Versions of the Self: Studies in English Autobiography from John Bunyan to John Stuart Mill.* New York: Basic Books, 1966.

1157 MUELLER, Iris W. *John Stuart Mill and French Thought.* Urbana: University of Illinois Press, 1956.

1158 NEFF, Emery E. *Carlyle and Mill.* See **529.**

1159 PACKE, Michael St. John. *The Life of John Stuart Mill.* New York: Macmillan, 1954.*

1160 PANKHURST, Richard K. P. *The Saint Simonians, Mill and Carlyle: A Perface to Modern Thought.* London: Sidgwick and Jackson, 1957.

1161 ROBSON, John M. "J. S. Mill's Theory of Poetry." *University of Toronto Quarterly,* XXIX (1960), 420–438.

1162 ROBSON, John M. "Mill's Autobiography: The Public and the Private Voice." *College Composition and Communication,* XVI (1965), 97–101.

1163 ROBSON, John M. *The Improvement of Mankind: The Social and Political Thought of John Stuart Mill.* Toronto: University of Toronto Press, 1968.*

1164 ROBSON, John M. "John Stuart Mill." See **67.**

1165 RYAN, Alan. *John Stuart Mill.* New York: Pantheon, 1970.*

1166 SHARPLESS, F. P. *The Literary Criticism of John Stuart Mill.* The Hague: Mouton, 1967.

1167 SIMON, Walter M. *European Positivism in the Nineteenth Century.* Ithaca: Cornell University Press, 1963.

1168 STEPHEN, Leslie. *The English Utilitarians.* London: Duckworth, 1900.

1169 TATALOVICH, Anne. "John Stuart Mill: *The Subjection of Women*—an Analysis." *Southern Quarterly,* XII (1973), 87–105.

1170 THOMAS, William. " John Stuart Mill and the Uses of Autobiography." *History,* LVI (1971), 341–359.

1171 WARD, John W. "Mill, Marx, and Modern Individualism." *Virginia Quarterly Review,* XXXV (1959), 527–539.

1172 WOODS, Thomas. *Poetry and Philosophy: A Study in the Thought of John Stuart Mill.* London: Hutchinson, 1961.

Morris, William (1834–1896)

Editions

1173 MORRIS, May, ed. *Collected Works,* 24 vols. London: Longmans, 1910–1915. [Reprinted 1966.]

1174 MORRIS, May, ed. *William Morris, Artist, Writer, Socialist: Unpublished and Hitherto Inaccessible Writings.* Oxford: Blackwell, 1936.

1175 BRIGGS, Asa, ed. *William Morris: Selected Writings and Designs*. Baltimore: Penguin Books, 1962.

1176 COLE, G. D. H., ed. *William Morris: Selected Writings*, Centenary Edition. New York: Random House, 1942.

1177 HENDERSON, Philip, ed. *The Letters of William Morris to His Family and Friends*. New York: Longmans, 1950.

1178 LE MIRE, Eugene D., ed. *The Unpublished Lectures of William Morris*. Detroit: Wayne State University Press, 1969.

Biography

1179 BLOOMFIELD, Paul. *The Life and Work of William Morris*. London: Barker, 1934.

1180 CLUTTON-BROCK, Arthur. *William Morris: His Work and Influence*. New York: Holt, 1914.

1181 COMPTON-RICKETT, Arthur. *William Morris: A Study in Personality*. London: Jenkins, 1913.

1182 ESHLEMAN, Lloyd W. *A Victorian Rebel: The Life of William Morris*. New York: Scribner, 1940. [Same book reissued under name of Lloyd Eric Grey in 1949 as *William Morris, Prophet of England's New Order*.]

1183 GLASIER, John B. *William Morris and the Early Days of the Socialist Movement*. New York: Longmans, 1921.

1184 HENDERSON, Philip. *William Morris: His Life, Work and Friends*. New York: McGraw Hill, 1967.*

1185 MACKAIL, John W. *The Life of William Morris*, 2 vols. New York: Longmans, 1922. [Also in World's Classics, #521.]*

1186 MACKAIL, John W. *William Morris and His Circle*. London: Oxford University Press, 1907.

1187 MEYNELL, Esther. *Portrait of William Morris*. London: Chapman, 1947.

1188 SHAW, George Bernard. *William Morris as I Knew Him*. New York: Dodd Mead, 1936.

1189 THOMPSON, Edward P. *William Morris, Romantic to Revolutionary*. New York: Monthly Review Press, 1962.*

1190 WEEKLEY, Montague. *William Morris*. London: Duckworth, 1934.

Criticism

1191 ANTIPPAS, Andy P. "William Morris and 'The Murder of Art.' " *Tulane Studies in English*, XVI (1968), 49–62.

1192 ARNOT, R. Page. *William Morris, the Man and the Myth*. London: Lawrence Wishart, 1964. [On Morris as a Socialist.]

1193 BERRY, Ralph. "A Defense of *Guenevere*." *Victorian Poetry*, IX (1971), 277–286.

1194 BLENCH, J. W. "William Morris's *Sigurd the Volsung:* A Reappraisal." *Durham University Journal*, XXX (1969), 1–17.

1195 BRANTLINGER, Patrick. "A Reading of Morris' *The Defence of Guenevere and Other Poems*." *Victorian Newsletter*, #44 (Fall, 1973), 18–24.

1196 CALHOUN, Blue. *The Pastoral Vision of William Morris*. Athens: University of Georgia Press, 1975.

1197 CARSON, Mother Angela. "Morris' Guenevere: A Further Note." *Philological Quarterly*, XLII (1963), 131–134.

1198 CHESTERTON, G. K. "William Morris and His School," *Varied Types*. New York: Dodd Mead, 1903.

1199 EHRSAM, T. G., *et al. Bibliographies*. See **72.**

1200 ELLISON, R. C. " 'The Undying Glory of Dreams': William Morris and the 'Northland of Old.' " See **49.**

1201 EVANS, B. I. *William Morris and His Poetry*. London: Harrap, 1925.

1202 FAULKNER, Peter, ed. *William Morris: The Critical Heritage*. London: Routledge Kegan Paul, 1973.

1203 FREDEMAN, William E. "The Pre-Raphaelites: William Morris." See **81.**

1204 GOODE, John. "Gissing, Morris and English Socialism." *Victorian Studies*, XII (1968), 201–226.

1205 GRENNAN, M. R. *William Morris, Medievalist and Revolutionary*. New York: King's Crown Press, 1945.

1206 HERFORD, C. H. *Norse Myth in English Poetry*. London: Longmans, 1919.

1207 HOARE, D. M. *The Works of Morris and Yeats in Relation to Early Saga Literature*. New York: Macmillan, 1937.

1208 HOUGH, Graham. *The Last Romantics*. See **94.**

1209 JACKSON, Holbrook. *William Morris, Craftsman-Socialist*. London: Cape, 1926.

1210 JAMES, Henry. "The Poetry of William Morris," *Views and Reviews*. Boston: Ball, 1908.

1211 LEWIS, C. S. *Rehabilitations*. London: Oxford University Press, 1939.

1212 LUBBOCK, Percy. "The Poetry of William Morris." *Quarterly Review*, CCXV (1911), 482–504.

1213 MACKAIL, John W. "William Morris," *Studies of English Poets*. London: Longmans, 1926.

1214 MAURER, Oscar. "Morris's Treatment of Greek Legend in *The Earthly Paradise*." *University of Texas Studies in English*, XXXIII (1954), 103–118.

1215 MAURER, Oscar. "William Morris and *Laxdoela Saga*." *Texas Studies in Literature and Language*, V (1963), 422–437.

1216 MAURER, Oscar. "William Morris and the Poetry of Escape," *Nineteenth Century Studies*, ed. by Herbert Davis. Ithaca, N.Y.: Cornell University Press, 1940.

1217 PARRY, J. J. "Note on the Prosody of William Morris." *Modern Language Notes*, XLIV (1929), 306–309.

1218 PATER, Walter. "Aesthetic Poetry," *Appreciations*. London: Macmillan, 1889.

1219 PATRICK, John M. "Morris and Froissart: 'Geffray Teste Noire' and 'The Haystack in the Floods.' " *Notes and Queries*, n.s., V (1958), 425–427.

1220 PERRINE, Laurence. "Morris's Guenevere: An Interpretation." *Philological Quarterly*, XXXIX (1960), 234–241.

1221 PHELAN, Mrs. A. A. *The Social Philosophy of William Morris*. Durham, N.C.: Duke University Press, 1927.

1222 RAYMOND, Meredith B. "The Arthurian Group in *The Defence of Guenevere and Other Poems*." *Victorian Poetry*, IV (1966), 213–218.

1223 SCOTT, Temple. *A Bibliography of the Works of William Morris*. London: Bell, 1897.

1224 SEWTER, A. Charles. *The Stained Glass of William Morris and His Circle*. New Haven: Yale University Press, 1974.

1225 SILVER, Carole G. " 'The Defence of Guenevere': A Further Interpretation." *Studies in English Literature*, IX (1969), 695–702.

1226 SPARLING, Henry H. *The Kelmscott Press and William Morris, Master-Craftsman*. London: Macmillan, 1924.

1227 STAINES, David. "Morris' Treatment of His Medieval Sources in *The Defence of Guenevere and Other Poems*." *Studies in Philology*, LXX (1973), 439–464.

1228 STALLMAN, Robert L. " 'Rapunzel' Unravelled." *Victorian Poetry*, VII (1969), 221–232.

1229 SYMONS, Arthur. "William Morris," *Studies in Two Literatures*. London: Secker, 1924.

1230 THOMPSON, Paul. *The Work of William Morris*. New York: Viking, 1967.*

1231 TOMPKINS, J. M. S. "The Work of William Morris: A Cord of Triple Strand." *Dalhousie Review*, L (1970), 97–111.

1232 VON HENDY, Andrew. "Histories and Flowers: The Organic Unity of William Morris' Late Art." *Victorian Newsletter*, #32 (Fall, 1967), 18–19.

1233 WAHL, John Robert. *No Idle Singer*. Cape Town: Balkema, 1964.

1234 WATKINSON, Ray. *William Morris as Designer*. London: Studio Vista, 1967.

1235 WILSON, S. P. "William Morris and France." *South Atlantic Quarterly*, XXIII (1924), 242–255.

1236 YEATS, William Butler. "The Happiest of the Poets," *Ideas of Good and Evil*. London: Bullen, 1903.

Newman, John Henry (1801–1890)

Editions

1237 *Collected Works*, 40 vols. New York: Longmans, 1874–1921.

1238 HARROLD, Charles F., ed. *Apologia pro Vita Sua*. New York: Longmans, 1947.

1239 HARROLD, Charles F., ed. *Essays and Sketches*, 3 vols. New York: Longmans, 1948.

1240 HARROLD, Charles F., ed. *The Idea of a University*. New York: Longmans, 1947.

1241 DESSAIN, Charles Stephen, and Vincent Ferrer BLEHL, eds. *Letters and Diaries*, about 30 vols. London: Nelson, 1961 + (in progress).*

1242 BLEHL, Vincent Ferrer, ed. *The Essential Newman*. New York: New Ameri-can Library, 1963. [Mentor-Omega MT488.]

1243 TILLOTSON, Geoffrey, ed. *Newman: Prose and Poetry*. London: Hart-Davis, 1957.

1244 TRISTRAM, H., ed. *Newman: Autobiographical Writings*. London: Sheed and Ward, 1956.

1245 CULLER, A Dwight, ed. *Apologia pro Vita Sua*. Boston: Houghton Mifflin, 1956. [Riverside Editions B10.]

1246 SVAGLIC, Martin J., ed. *Apologia pro Vita Sua*. Oxford: Clarendon Press, 1967.

1247 DE LAURA, David J., ed. *Apologia pro Vita Sua*. New York: Norton, 1968. [Norton Critical Edition paperback; text background materials, criticism.]

Biography

1248 BOUYER, Louis. *Newman: His Life and Spirituality*. New York: Meridian Books, 1960.

1249 CROSS, Frank Leslie. *John Henry Newman*. London: Allan, 1933.

1250 DESSAIN, Charles Stephen. *John Henry Newman*. Stanford: Stanford University Press, 1971. [Especially on Newman's religious life.]*

1251 DE VERE, Aubrey. "Some Recollections of Cardinal Newman." *Nineteenth Century*, XL (1896), 395–411.

1252 FABER, Geoffrey. *Oxford Apostles*. London: Faber, 1933.

1253 HUTTON, Richard Holt. *Cardinal Newman*. Boston: Houghton Mifflin, 1iox.

1254 MIDDLETON, R. D. *Newman at Oxford: His Religious Development*. London: Oxford University Press, 1950.

1255 ROBBINS, William. *The Newman Brothers: An Essay in Comparative Biography*. Cambridge: Harvard University Press, 1966.*

1256 RUGGLES, Eleanor. *Journey into Faith*. New York: Norton, 1944.

1257 TREVOR, Meriol. *Newman: Light in Winter*. New York: Doubleday, 1963.

1258 TREVOR, Meriol. *Newman: The Pillar of the Cloud*. New York: Doubleday, 1962.

1259 WARD, Maisie. *Young Mr. Newman*. New York: Sheed and Ward, 1948.

1260 WARD, Wilfrid. *The Life of John Henry, Cardinal Newman*, 2 vols. London: Longmans, 1912.*

Criticism

1261 ALTHOLZ, Josef L. "Newman and History." *Victorian Studies*, VII (1964), 285–294.

1262 BLEHL, Vincent Ferrer. *Newman's Apologia: A Classic Reconsidered*. New York: Harcourt Brace, 1964.

1263 BLEHL, Vincent Ferrer. "Newman, the Fathers, and Education." *Thought*, XLV (1970), 196–212.

1264 BOKENKOTTER, Thomas S. *Cardinal Newman as an Historian*. Louvain: Bibliothèque de l'Université, 1959.

1265 CAMERON, James Munro. *The Night Battle*. London: Burns and Oates, 1962. [Includes an essay on Newman and empiricism.]

1266 CHURCH, Richard W. *The Oxford Movement*. London: Macmillan, 1894.

1267 COULSON, John. *Newman and the Common Tradition: A Study in the Language of Church and Society*. New York: Oxford University Press, 1970.

JOHN HENRY NEWMAN

1268 CRONIN, J. F. *Cardinal Newman: His Theory of Knowledge.* Washington, D.C.: Catholic University of America Press, 1935.

1269 CULLER, A. Dwight. *The Imperial Intellect.* New Haven: Yale University Press, 1955.* [On Newman's theory of education.]

1270 DALE, Peter A. "Newman's *The Idea of a University:* The Dangers of a University Education." *Victorian Studies,* XVI (1972), 5–36.

1271 DEEN, Leonard W. "The Rhetoric of Newman's *Apologia.*" *ELH,* XXIX (1962), 224–238.

1272 DE LAURA, David J. *Hebrew and Hellene in Victorian England.* See **224.**

1273 DESSAIN, Charles Stephen. "Newman's Philosophy and Theology." See **67.** [A close review of materials largely omitted from this bibliography.]

1274 HARROLD, Charles F. *John Henry Newman.* New York: Longmans, 1945.*

1275 HOLLIS, Christopher. *Newman and the Modern World.* New York: Doubleday, 1968.

1276 HOUGHTON, Walter E. *The Art of Newman's Apologia.* New Haven: Yale University Press, 1945.*

1277 HUTTON, Richard Holt. "Two Great Oxford Thinkers: Cardinal Newman and Matthew Arnold." See **260.**

1278 KENNY, Terence. *The Political Thought of John Henry Newman.* London: Longmans, 1957.

1279 LAPATI, Americo D. *John Henry Newman.* New York: Twayne, 1972.

1280 McGRATH, Fergal. *The Consecration of Learning: Lectures on Newman's Idea of a University.* New York: Fordham University Press, 1963.

1281 McGRATH, Fergal. *Newman's University: Idea and Reality.* London: Longmans, 1951.

1282 PICK, John. "Newman the Poet." *Renascence,* VIII (1956), 127–135.

1283 RYAN, J. K., and E. D. BERNARD, eds. *American Essays for the Newman Centennial.* Washington, D.C.: Catholic University of America Press, 1947.

1284 SVAGLIC, Martin J. "John Henry Newman." See **67.**

1285 SVAGLIC, Martin J. "The Structure of Newman's *Apologia.*" See **155.**

1286 THIRLWALL, John C. "John Henry Newman: His Poetry and His Conversion." *Dublin Review,* CCXLII (1968), 75–88.

1287 VARGISH, Thomas. *Newman: The Contemplation of Mind.* New York: Oxford University Press, 1970.*

1288 WALGRAVE, J. H. *Newman the Theologian.* New York: Sheed and Ward, 1960.

1289 WAMSLEY, Geoffrey. "Newman's *Dream of Gerontius.*" *Downside Review,* XCI (1973), 167–185.

1290 WEATHERBY, Harold L. *Cardinal Newman in His Age.* Nashville: Vanderbilt University Press, 1973.*

1291 WEBB, C. C. J. *Religious Thought in the Oxford Movement.* New York: Macmillan, 1928.

Pater, Walter
(1839–1894)

Editions

1292 *Works,* 10 vols. London: Macmillan, 1910.

1293 EVANS, Lawrence, ed. *Letters of Walter Pater.* New York: Oxford University Press, 1970.*

1294 ALDINGTON, Richard, ed. *Selected Works.* London: Heinemann, 1951.

1295 PATMORE, Derek, ed. *Selected Writings.* London: Falcon Press, 1949.

1296 *Marius the Epicurean.* New York: Modern Library, n.d.

1297 *The Renaissance.* New York: Modern Library, n.d.

Biography and Criticism

1298 BAKER, Joseph E. "Ivory Tower as Laboratory: Pater and Proust." *Accent,* XIX (1959), 204–216.

1299 BENSON, Arthur C. *Walter Pater.* New York: Macmillan, 1906.

1300 BRZENK, Eugene. "The Unique Fictional World of Walter Pater." *Nineteenth Century Fiction,* XIII (1958), 217–226.

1301 CECIL, Lord David. *The Fine Art of Reading and Other Literary Studies.* London: Constable, 1957.

1302 CHILD, Ruth. *The Aesthetic of Walter Pater.* New York: Macmillan, 1940.

1303 CRINKLEY, Richmond. *Walter Pater: Humanist.* Lexington: University of Kentucky Press, 1970.

1304 DE LAURA, David J. *Hebrew and Hellene in Victorian England.* See **224.**

1305 DE LAURA, David J. "The 'Wordsworth' of Pater and Arnold." See **227.**

1306 D'HANGEST, Germain. *Walter Pater: l'homme et l'oeuvre,* 2 vols. Paris: Didier, 1962.

1307 DOWNES, David A. *The Temper of Victorian Belief: Studies in the Religious Novels of Pater, Kingsley and Newman.* New York: Twayne, 1972.

1308 DOWNES, David A. *Victorian Portraits: Hopkins and Pater.* See **878.**

1309 DUFFY, John J. "Walter Pater's Prose Style: an Essay in Theory and Analysis." *Style,* I (1967), 45–63.

1310 EAKER, J. G. *Walter Pater: A Study in Methods and Effects.* Iowa City: University of Iowa, 1933.

1311 EVANS, Lawrence. "Walter Pater." See **67.**

1312 FLETCHER, Ian. *Walter Pater.* London: Longmans, 1959.

1313 HARRIS, Wendell V. "Pater as Prophet." *Criticism,* VI (1964), 349–360.

1314 HOUGH, Graham. *The Last Romantics.* See **94.**

1315 JOHNSON, R. V. *Walter Pater: a Study of his Critical Outlook and Achievement.* Victoria, Australia: Melbourne University Press, 1961.

1316 KNOEPFLMACHER, U. C. *Religious Humanism and the Victorian Novel: George Eliot, Walter Pater, and Samuel Butler.* Princeton: Princeton University Press, 1965.*

1317 LENAGHAN, R. T. "Pattern in Walter Pater's Fiction." *Studies in Philolgy,* LVIII (1961), 69–91.

1318 McKENZIE, Gordon. *The Literary Character of Walter Pater.* Berkeley: University of California Press, 1967.

1319 MASON, Mary G. "Wordsworth and Pater's First Imaginary Portrait." *Harvard Library Bulletin,* XIX (1971), 195–203.

1320 MONSMAN, Gerald C. *Pater's Portraits: Mythic Pattern in the Fiction of Walter Pater.* Baltimore: Johns Hopkins Press, 1967.*

1321 MONSMAN, Gerald C., and Samuel WRIGHT. "Walter Pater: Style and Text." *South Atlantic Quarterly,* LXXI (1972), 108–123.

1322 PIERLE, Robert C. "Walter Pater and Epicureanism." *Southern Quarterly,* VII (1969), 131–140.

1323 ROSENBLATT, Louise M. "The Genesis of Pater's *Marius the Epicurean.*" *Comparative Literature,* XIV (1963), 242–260.

1324 SUDRANN, Jean. "Victorian Compromise and Modern Revolution." *ELH,* XXVI (1959), 425–444. [On *Marius*.]

1325 SYMONS, Arthur. *A Study of Walter Pater.* London: Sawyer, 1932.

1326 WARD, Anthony. *Walter Pater: the Idea in Nature.* London: MacGibbon and Kee, 1966.

1327 WELLEK, René. "Walter Pater's Literary Theory and Criticism." *Victorian Studies,* I (1957), 29–46.

1328 WEST, Paul. "Pater and the Tribulations of Taste." *University of Toronto Quarterly,* XXVII (1958), 424–433.

1329 WRIGHT, Thomas. *The Life of Walter Pater,* 2 vols. New York: Putnam, 1907.

1330 YOUNG, Helen H. *The Writings of Walter Pater, a Reflection of British Philosophical Opinions from 1860–1890,* Lancaster, Pa.: Lancaster Press, 1933.*

Patmore, Coventry
(1823–1896)

Editions

1331 *Works,* 5 vols. London: Bell, 1907.

1332 PAGE, Frederick, ed. The Poems. New York: Oxford University Press, 1949.

1333 PATMORE, Derek, ed. *A Selection of Poems.* London: Grey Walls Press, 1948.

Biography and Criticism

1334 BURDETT, Osbert. *The Idea of Coventry Patmore.* London: Oxford University Press, 1921.

1335 CADBURY, William. "The Structure of Feeling in a Poem by Patmore." *Victorian Poetry,* IV (1966), 237–251.

1336 CHAMPNEYS, Basil. *Memoirs and Correspondence of Coventry Patmore.* London: Bell, 1900.

1337 CHURCH, Richard W. "The Devout Amorist." *Spectator,* CXLI (1928), 237–238.

1338 DE VERE, Aubrey. "Coventry Patmore's Poetry," *Essays Chiefly Literary and Ethical.* London: Macmillan, 1889.

1339 DUNN, John J. "Love and Eroticism: Coventry Patmore's Mystical Imagery." *Victorian Poetry,* VII (1969), 203–219.

1340 GARDNER, W. H. "The Status of Coventry Patmore." *Month,* XX (1958), 205–219.

1341 GOSSE, Edmund. *Coventry Patmore.* New York: Scribner, 1905.

1342 HOLLOWAY, John. "Patmore, Donne, and the 'Wit of Love,' " *The Charted Mirror.* London: Routledge, 1960.

1343 LOHRLI, Anne. "Coventry Patmore in *Household Words." Victorian Newsletter,* #31 (Spring 1967), 25–27.

1344 LUBBOCK, Percy. "The Poetry of Patmore." *Quarterly Review,* CCVIII (1908), 356–376.

1345 McELRATH, Joseph R. "Coventry Patmore's 'The Angel in the House': the Experience of Divine Love." *Cithara,* X, i (1970), 45–53.

1346 OLIVER, Edward James. *Coventry Patmore.* New York: Sheed and Ward, 1956.

1347 PAGE, Frederick. *Patmore: A Study in Poetry.* New York: Oxford University Press, 1933.*

1349 PRAZ, Mario. "The Epic of the Everyday," *The Hero in Eclipse in Victorian Fiction.* New York: Oxford University Press, 1956.

1350 READ, Herbert. "Coventry Patmore," *Collected Essays in Literary Criticism.* London: Faber, 1951.

1351 REID, John C. *The Mind and Art of Coventry Patmore.* New York: Macmillan, 1957.*

1352 SHUSTER, G. N. "Poetry and Three Poets," *The Catholic Spirit in Modern English Literature.* New York: Macmillan, 1922.

1353 STEVENSON, Lionel. "Coventry Patmore." See **81.**

1354 SYMONS, Arthur. "Coventry Patmore," *Studies in Two Literatures.* London: Secker, 1924.

1355 WHEATON, L. "Emily Honoria Patmore and Coventry Patmore's Poetry." *Dublin Review,* CLXIII (1918), 207–233.

Rossetti, Christina
(1830–1894)

Editions

1356 ROSSETTI, William Michael, ed. *Poetical Works.* London: Macmillan, 1924.

1357 *Goblin Market, the Prince's Progress, and Other Poems.* London: Oxford University Press, 1913. [World's Classics.]

1358 ROSSETTI, William Michael, ed. *Family Letters of Christina Georgina Rossetti.* New York: Scribner, 1908.

1359 TROXELL, Janet C. *Three Rossettis: Unpublished Letters to and from Dante Gabriel, Christina, William.* Cambridge: Harvard University Press, 1937.

Biography

1360 BELL, H. T. Mackenzie. *Christina Rossetti: A Biographical and Critical Study.* Boston: Roberts, 1898.

1361 CARY, Elisabeth L. *The Rossettis: Dante Gabriel and Christina.* New York: Putnam, 1900.

1362 PACKER, Lona Mosk. *Christina Rossetti.* Berkeley: University of California Press, 1963.*

1363 SANDARS, Mary F. *The Life of Christina Rossetti.* London: Hutchinson, 1930.

1364 SAWTELL Margaret. *Christina Rossetti: Her Life and Religion.* London: Mowbray, 1955.

1365 ZATURENSKA, Marya. *Christina Rossetti: A Portrait with Background.* New York: Macmillan, 1949.

Criticism

1366 ADLARD, John. "Christina Rossetti: Strategies of Loneliness." *Contemporary Review*, CCXXI (1972), 146–150.

1367 BENSON, Arthur C. "Christina Rossetti," *Essays.* New York: Macmillan, 1896.

1368 BIRKHEAD, Edith. *Christina Rossetti and Her Poetry.* London: Harrap, 1930.

1369 DE VITIS, A. A. "*Goblin Market:* Fairy Tale and Reality." *Journal of Popular Culture,* I (1968), 418–426.

1370 EHRSAM, T. G. *et al. Bibliographies.* See **72.**

1371 FESTA, Conrad. "Symbol and Meaning in 'A Birthday.' " *English Language Notes,* XI (1973), 50–56.

1372 HÖNNIGHAUSEN, Gisela. "Emblematic Tendencies in the Works of Christina Rossetti." *Victorian Poetry,* X (1972), 1–15.

1373 JANOWITZ, K. E. "The Antipodes of Self: Three Poems by Christina Rossetti." *Victorian Poetry,* XI (1973), 195–205.

1374 LOWTHER, George. "Christina Rossetti." *Contemporary Review,* CIV (1913), 681–689.

1375 MEYNELL, Alice. "Christina Rossetti." *New Review,* XII (1895), 201–206.

1376 MORE, Paul Elmer. "Christina Rossetti," *Shelburne Essays,* Third Series. New York: Putnam, 1907.

1377 NOBLE, James A. "The Burden of Christina Rossetti," *Impressions and Memories.* London: Dent, 1895.

1378 SHOVE, Fredegond. *Christina Rossetti: A Study.* New York: Macmillan, 1931.

1379 SWANN, Thomas B. *Wonder and Whimsy: The Fantastic World of Christina Rossetti.* London: Marshall Jones, 1960.

1380 THOMAS, Eleanor W. *Christina Georgina Rossetti.* New York: Columbia University Press, 1931.

1381 WEATHERS, Winston. "Christina Rossetti: The Sisterhood of Self." *Victorian Poetry,* III (1965), 81–89.

Rossetti, Dante Gabriel (1828–1882)

See also items concerning the *Pre-Raphaelites* under "General Studies," especially **42, 49, 60, 86, 90, 92, 94, 150,** and **162, 169.**

Editions

1382 ROSSETTI, William Michael, ed. *Works,* The Siddal Edition, 7 vols. London: Ellis, 1900–1901.

1383 ROSSETTI, William Michael, ed. *Complete Poetical Works.* Boston: Little Brown, 1903.

1384 ROSSETTI, William Michael, ed. *Family Letters,* 2 vols. London: Ellis, 1895.

1385 ROSSETTI, William Michael, ed. *The Germ.* London: Stock, 1901. [A reprint of the Pre-Raphaelite "little magazine" of 1850.]

1386 ROSSETTI, William Michael, ed. *Rossetti Papers, 1862 to 1870.* London: Sands, 1902.

1387 ROSSETTI, William Michael, ed. *Pre-Raphaelite Diaries and Letters.* London: Hurst, 1900.

1388 BAUM, Paull F., ed. *Letters to Fanny Cornforth.* Baltimore: Johns Hopkins Press, 1940.

1389 DOUGHTY, Oswald, and John Robert WAHL, eds. *Letters of Dante Gabriel Rossetti,* 4 vols. London: Loford University Press, 1965–1966.

1390 BAUM, Paull, F., ed. *The House of Life.* Cambridge: Harvard University Press, 1928.

1391 BAUM, Paull F., ed. *Poems, Ballads and Sonnets.* New York: Doubleday, 1937.

1392 HOSMON, Robert S., ed. *The Germ: A Pre-Raphaelite Little Magazine.* Coral Gables, Florida: University of Miami Press, 1970.

Biography

1393 ADRIAN, Arthur A. "The Browning-Rossetti Friendship: Some Unpublished Letters." *PMLA,* LXXIII (1958), 538–544.

1394 ANGELI, Helen R. *Dante Gabriel Rossetti, His Friends and Enemies.* London: Hamilton, 1949.

1395 BEERBOHM, Max. *Rossetti and His Circle.* London: Heinemann, 1922. [Carricatures.]*

1396 BURNE-JONES, Georgiana, ed. *Memorials of Edward Burne-Jones,* 2 vols. New York: Macmillan, 1904.

DANTE GABRIEL ROSSETTI

1397 CAINE, Hall. *Recollections of Rossetti.* New York: Cassell, 1928.

1398 DOUGHTY, Oswald. *Dante Gabriel Rossetti, a Victorian Romantic.* New Haven: Yale University Press, 1960.*

1399 DUNN, H. T. *Recollections of Dante Gabriel Rossetti and His Circle.* London: Mathews, 1904.

1400 FREDEMAN, William E. *Prelude to the Last Decade.* Manchester: John Rylands Library, 1971.

1401 GILCHRIST, H. H. "Recollections of Rossetti." *Lippincott's Magazine,* LXVIII (1901), 571–576.

1402 GRYLLS, Rosalie Glynn. *Portrait of Rossetti.* London: Macdonald, 1964.

1403 HUNT, Violet. *The Wife of Rossetti.* New York: Dutton, 1932.

1404 HUNT, W. Holman. *Pre-Raphaelitism and the Pre-Raphaelite Brotherhood,* New York: Dutton, 1914.*

1405 MARILLIER, H. C. *Dante Gabriel Rossetti: An Illustrated Memorial of His Art and Life.* London: Bell, 1890.

1406 PEDRICK, Gale. *Life with Rossetti, or No Peacocks Allowed.* London: Macdonald, 1964.

1407 ROSSETTI, William Michael. *Dante Gabriel Rossetti as Designer and Writer.* London: Cassell, 1889.

1408 ROSSETTI, William Michael, ed. *Ruskin: Rossetti: Pre-Raphaelitism: Papers, 1854–1861.* New York: Dodd Mead, 1899.

1409 WAUGH, Evelyn. *Rossetti: His Life and Works.* London: Duckworth, 1928.

1410 WINWAR, Frances. *Poor Splendid Wings: The Rossettis and Their Circle.* Boston: Little Brown, 1933.

1411 WOOD, Esther. *Dante Rossetti and the Pre-Raphaelite Movement.* London: Low, 1894.

Criticism

1412 BAKER, Houston A., Jr. "The Poet's Progress: Rossetti's *The House of Life.*" *Victorian Poetry,* VIII (1970), 1–14.

1413 BARTH, J. Robert, S. J. "Mysticism in Rossetti's *House of Life.*" *Barat Review,* VI (1971), 41–48.

1414 BOWRA, C. M. "The House of Life," *The Romantic Imagination.* Cambridge: Harvard University Press, 1947.

1415 BUCHANAN, Robert W. "The Fleshly School of Poetry." *Contemporary Review,* XVIII (1871), 334–350. [Expanded as *The Fleshly School of Poetry and Other Phenomena of the Day.* London: Strahan, 1872.]

1416 BUCKLEY, Jerome H. "Pre-Raphaelite Past and Present: The Poetry of the Rossettis." See **49.**

1417 BURGUM, E. B. "Rossetti and the Ivory Tower." *Sewanee Review,* XXXVII (1929), 431–446.

1418 CASSIDY, John A. "Robert Buchanan and the Fleshly Controversy." *PMLA,* LXVII (1952), 65–93.

1419 COOPER, Robert M. *Lost on Both Sides: Dante Gabriel Rossetti, Critic and Poet.* Athens: Ohio University Press, 1970.

1420 EHRSAM, T. G., *et al. Bibliographies.* See **72.**

DANTE GABRIEL ROSSETTI

1421 FLEMING, G. H. *Rossetti and the Pre-Raphaelite Brotherhood*. London: Hart-Davis, 1967.

1422 FLEMING, G. H. *That Ne'er Shall Meet Again: Rossetti, Millais, Hunt*. London: Joseph, 1969.

1423 FORD, George H. *Keats and the Victorians*. See **83**.

1424 FRASER, Robert S., ed. *Essays on the Rossettis*. Princeton: Princeton University Library, 1972.

1425 FREDEMAN, William E. "The Pre-Raphaelites." See **81**.

1426 FREDEMAN, William E. *Pre-Raphaelitism: A Bibliocritical Study*. Cambridge: Harvard University Press, 1965.*

1427 FREDEMAN, William E. "Rossetti's 'In Memoriam': An Elegiac Reading of *The House of Life*." *Bulletin of John Rylands Library*, XLVII (1965), 298–341.

1428 HAMILTON, Walter. *The Aesthetic Movement in England*. London: Reeves, 1882.

1429 HARRIS, Wendell V. "A Reading of Rossetti's Lyrics." *Victorian Poetry*, VII (1971), 299–308.

1430 HOWARD, Ronnalie Roper. *The Dark Glass: Vision and Technique in the Poetry of Dante Gabriel Rossetti*. Athens: Ohio University Press, 1972.*

1431 HUNT, John Dixon. *The Pre-Raphaelite Imagination*. Lincoln: University of Nebraska Press, 1969.*

1432 HYDER, Clyde K. "Rossetti's *Rose Mary*: A Study in the Occult." *Victorian Poetry*, I (1963), 197–207.

1433 JOHNSON, Wendell Stacy. "D. G. Rossetti as Painter and Poet." *Victorian Poetry*, III (1965), 9–18.

1434 JOHNSTON, Robert D. *Dante Gabriel Rossetti*. New York: Twayne, 1969.

1435 KNICKERBOCKER, Kenneth L. "Rossetti's 'The Blessed Damozel.'" *Studies in Philology*, XXIX (1932), 485–504.

1436 McGANN, Jerome J. "Rossetti's Significant Details." *Victorian Poetry*, VII (1969), 41–54.

1437 MÉGROZ, R. L. *Dante Gabriel Rossetti, Painter Poet of Heaven in Earth*. London: Faber, 1928.

1438 MYERS, F. W. H. "Rossetti and the Religion of Beauty," *Essays, Modern*. London: Macmillan, 1908.

1439 NICOLL, John. *The Pre-Raphaelites*. London: Studio Vista, 1970. [The paintings.]

1440 PATER, Walter. "Dante Gabriel Rossetti," *Appreciations*. London: Macmillan, 1889.

1441 PETERSON, Carl A. "Rossetti's 'A Last Confession' as Dramatic Monologue." *Victorian Poetry*, XI (1973), 127–142.

1442 ROBERTS, Helene E. "The Dream World of Dante Gabriel Rossetti." *Victorian Studies*, XVII (1974), 371–393.

1443 ROBILLARD, Douglas J. "Rossetti's 'Willowwood Sonnets' and the Structure of *The House of Life*." *Victorian Newsletter*, #22 (1962), 5–9.

1444 ROSSETTI, William Michael. *Bibliography of the Works of Dante Gabriel Rossetti*. London: Ellis, 1905.

1445 RYALS, Clyde de L. "The Narrative Unity of *The House of Life*." *Journal of English and Germanic Philology*, LXXIX (1970), 241–257.

1446 SAVARIT, Jacques. *Tendances mystiques et ésotériques chez Dante-Gabriel Rossetti*. Paris: Didier, 1961.

1447 SHINE, Hill. "The Influence of Keats upon Rossetti." *Englische Studien,* LXI (1927), 183–210.

1448 SONSTROEM, David. *Rossetti and the Fair Lady.* Middletown, Conn.: Wesleyan University Press, 1970.

1449 SPECTOR, Stephen J. "Love, Unity, and Desire in the Poetry of Dante Gabriel Rossetti." *ELH,* XXXVIII (1971), 432–458.

1450 STEIN, Richard L. "Dante Gabriel Rossetti: Painting and the Problem of Poetic Form." *Studies in English Literature,* X (1970), 776–792.

1451 STEVENSON, Lionel. *The Pre-Raphaelite Poets.* Chapel Hill: University of North Carolina Press, 1972.

1452 SURTEES, Virginia. *The Paintings and Drawings of Dante Gabriel Rossetti: A Catalogue Raisonné,* 2 vols. London: Oxford University Press, 1971.*

1453 SYMONS, Arthur. "Dante Gabriel Rossetti." *Figures of Several Centuries.* London: Constable, 1916.

1454 TURNER, F. M. "Rossetti's Reading and His Critical Opinions." *PMLA,* XLII (1927), 465–491.

1455 VOGEL, Joseph F. *Dante Gabriel Rossetti's Versecraft.* Gainesville: University of Florida Press, 1971.

1456 WALLERSTEIN, Ruth C. "Personal Experience in Rossetti's *House of Life.*" *PMLA,* XLII (1927), 492–504.

1457 WAUGH, Evelyn. "D. G. Rossetti: A Centenary Criticism." *Fortnightly Review,* CXXIX (1928), 595–604.

1458 WEATHERBY, Harold L. "Problems of Form and Content in the Poetry of Dante Gabriel Rossetti." *Victorian Poetry,* II (1964), 11–19.

1459 WILLOUGHBY, Leonard A. *Dante Gabriel Rosselli and German Literature.* London: Oxford University Press, 1912.

Ruskin, John
(1819–1900)

Editions

1460 COOK, E. T., and Alexander WEDDERBURN. *The Works of Ruskin,* 39 vols. London: Allen, 1903–1912.*

1461 EVANS, Joan, and J. H. WHITEHOUSE, eds. *The Diaries of John Ruskin,* 3 vols. Oxford: Clarendon Press, 1956–1959.

1462 BRADLEY, John Lewis, ed. *The Letters of John Ruskin to Lord and Lady Mount-Temple.* Columbus: Ohio State University Press, 1964.

1463 BRADLEY, John Lewis, ed. *Ruskin's Letters from Venice, 1851–1852.* New Haven: Yale University Press, 1955.

1464 NORTON, Charles Eliot, ed. *Letters of John Ruskin to Charles Eliot Norton,* 2 vols. Boston: Houghton Mifflin, 1905.

1465 BURD, Van Akin, ed. *The Ruskin Family Letters, 1801–1843,* 2 vols. Ithaca, N.Y.: Cornell University Press, 1973.

1466 BURD, Van Akin, ed. *The Winnington Letters: John Ruskin's Correspondence with Margaret Alexis Bell and the Children at Winnington Hall.* Cambridge: Harvard University Press, 1970.

1467 VILJOEN, Helen Gill, ed. *The Brantwood Diary of John Ruskin.* New Haven: Yale University Press, 1971.

1468 BALL, A. H. R., ed. *Ruskin as Literary Critic: Selections.* Cambridge: Cambridge University Press, 1928.

1469 BLOOM, Harold, ed. *The Literary Criticism of John Ruskin.* Garden City, N.Y.: Doubleday, 1965. [Anchor Books, A480.]

1470 EVANS, Joan, ed. *The Lamp of Beauty: Writings on Art by John Ruskin.* London: Phaidon Press, 1959.

1471 HERBERT, Robert L., ed. *The Art of Criticism of John Ruskin.* Garden City, N.Y.: Doubleday, 1964. [Anchor Books, A405]

1472 ROE, Frederick W., ed. *Selections and Essays.* New York: Scribner, 1918.

1473 ROSENBERG, John D., ed. *The Genius of John Ruskin: Selections.* New York: Braziller, 1963.

1474 CLARK, Kenneth, ed. *Ruskin Today.* New York: Holt, Rinehart and Winston, 1964.

Biography

1475 BENSON, Arthur C. *Ruskin: A Study in Personality.* London: Smith Elder, 1911.

1476 COLLINGWOOD, W. G. *The Life and Work of John Ruskin,* 2 vols. Boston: Houghton Mifflin, 1902.*

1477 COOK, E. T. *The Life of John Ruskin,* 2 vols. London: Allen, 1911.

1478 CROW, G. H. *Ruskin.* London: Duckworth, 1936.

1479 DEARDEN, James S., ed. *The Professor: Arthur Severn's Memoir of John Ruskin.* London: Allen and Unwin, 1967.

1480 EVANS, Joan. *John Ruskin.* New York: Oxford University Press, 1954.*

1481 HARRISON, Frederic. *John Ruskin.* New York: Macmillan, 1902.

1482 JAMES, Sir William, ed. *The Order of Release: The Story of John Ruskin, Effie Gray and John Everett Millais Told for the First Time in Their Unpublished Letters.* London: Murray, 1947.

1483 LEON, Derrick. *Ruskin: The Great Victorian.* London: Routledge Kegan Paul, 1949.*

1484 LUTYENS, Mary. *Millais and the Ruskins.* New York: Vanguard Press, 1969.

1485 QUENNELL, Peter. *John Ruskin: The Portrait of a Prophet.* New York: Viking, 1949.

1486 VILJOEN, Helen Gill. *Ruskin's Scottish Heritage: A Prelude.* Urbana: University of Illinois Press, 1951.*

1487 WHITEHOUSE, J. H. *Vindication of John Ruskin.* London: Allen, 1950.

1488 WILENSKI, R. H. *John Ruskin: An Introduction to Further Study of His Life and Work.* London: Faber, 1933.*

Criticism

1489 ALEXANDER, Edward. *Matthew Arnold, John Ruskin, and The Modern Temper.* See **202.**

JOHN RUSKIN

1490 ALEXANDER, Edward. "Ruskin and Science." *Modern Language Review,* LXIV (1969), 508–521.

1491 BALL, Patricia M. *The Science of Aspects.* See **865.**

1492 BRADLEY, John Lewis. *An Introduction to Ruskin.* Boston: Houghton Mifflin, 1971.

1493 BUCKLEY, Jerome H. "The Moral Aesthetic," *The Victorian Temper.* See **53.**

1494 BURD, Van Akin. "Background to Modern Painters: The Tradition and the Turner Controversy." *PMLA,* LXXIV (1959), 254–267.

1495 BURD, Van Akin. "Ruskin's Quest for a Theory of Imagination," *Modern Language Quarterly,* XVII (1956), 60–72.

1496 FAIN, John T. *Ruskin and the Economists.* Nashville: Vanderbilt University Press, 1956.

1497 FISHMAN, Solomon. *The Interpretation of Art: Essays on the Art Criticism of John Ruskin, Clive Bell, Roger Fry, Herbert Read.* Berkeley: University of California Press, 1963.

1498 FITCH, Raymond. *Life Against Wealth: Ruskin's Uses of Myth and Apocalypse.* Athens: Ohio University Press, 1970.

1499 FONTANEY, Pierre. "Ruskin and Paradise Regained." *Victorian Studies,* XII (1969), 347–356.

1500 GOETZ, Sister Mary Dorothea. *A Study of Ruskin's Concept of the Imagination.* Washington, D.C.: Catholic University of America, 1947.

1501 HERRMANN, Luke. *Ruskin and Turner.* London: Faber, 1968.

1502 HOUGH, Graham. "Ruskin," *The Last Romantics.* See **94.**

1503 JOSEPH, Robert J. "John Ruskin: Radical and Psychotic Genius." *Psychoanalytic Review,* LVI (1969), 425–441.

1504 LADD, Henry. *The Victorian Morality of Art: An Analysis of Ruskin's Esthetic.* New York: Long Smith, 1932.*

1505 LANDOW, George P. *The Aesthetic and Critical Theories of John Ruskin.* Princeton: Princeton University Press, 1971.*

1506 PAINTER, George D. *Proust: The Early Years.* Boston: Little Brown, 1959. [Contains material on Ruskin's influence on Proust.]

1507 ROE, Frederick W. *The Social Philosophy of Carlyle and Ruskin.* See **534.**

1508 ROSENBERG, John D. *The Darkening Glass: A Portrait of Ruskin's Genius.* New York: Columbia University Press, 1961.*

1509 ROSSETTI, William Michael. *Ruskin, Rossetti, Pre-Raphaelitism.* See **1408.**

1510 SHAW, George Bernard. *Ruskin's Politics.* London: Ruskin Centenary Council, 1921.

1511 SHERBURNE, James Clark. *John Ruskin, or The Ambiguities of Abundance: A Study in Social and Economic Criticism.* Cambridge: Harvard University Press, 1972.*

1512 STEIN, Roger B. *John Ruskin and Aesthetic Thought in America.* Cambridge: Harvard University Press, 1967.

1513 TOWNSEND, Francis G. "John Ruskin." See **67.**

1514 TOWNSEND, Francis G. *Ruskin and the Landscape Feeling.* Urbana: University of Illinois Press, 1951.

1515 WALTON, Paul H. *The Drawings of John Ruskin.* Oxford: Clarendon Press, 1972.

1516 WESLING, Donald. "Ruskin and the Adequacy of Landscape." *Texas Studies in Literature and Language*, IX (1967), 253–274.

1517 WHISTLER, J. A. M. *Whistler v. Ruskin*. London: Chatto and Windus, 1878.

1518 WHITEHOUSE, J. H., ed. *Ruskin the Prophet and Other Centenary Studies*. London: Allen and Unwin, 1920.

1519 WILLIAMS-ELLIS, Amabel. *The Tragedy of John Ruskin*. London: Cape, 1928.

Stevenson, Robert Louis (1850–1894)

Editions

1520 *Works*, South Seas Edition, 32 vols. New York: Scribner, 1925.

1521 SMITH, Janet Adam, ed. *Collected Poems*. London: Hart-Davis, 1971.*

1522 FERGUSON, De Lancey, and Marshall WAINGROW, eds. *RIS: Stevenson's Letters to Charles Baxter*. New Haven: Yale University Press, 1956.

1523 DAICHES, David, ed. *Robert Louis Stevenson: A Laurel Reader*. New York: Dell, 1959. [Dell paperback.]

1524 BOOTH, Bradford, ed. *Selected Poetry and Prose of Robert Louis Stevenson*. Boston: Houghton Mifflin, 1968. [Riverside Editions B111.]

1525 ELWIN, Malcolm, ed. *The Essays of Robert Louis Stevenson*. London: Macdonald, 1950.

1526 HART, James D., ed. *From Scotland to Silverado by Robert Louis Stevenson*. Cambridge: Harvard University Press, 1966.

Biography

1527 BALFOUR, Graham. *The Life of Robert Louis Stevenson*, 2 vols. New York: Scribner, 1901.*

1528 COHEN, Edward H. *The Henley-Stevenson Quarrel*. See **832.**

1529 COLVIN, Sidney. *Memories and Notes of Persons and Places*. New York: Scribner, 1921.

1530 FURNAS, J. C. *Voyage to Windward: The Life of Robert Louis Stevenson*. New York: Sloane, 1951.* [Apollo Books paperback.]

1531 MacKAY, Margaret. *The Violent Friend: The Story of Mrs. Robert Louis Stevenson*. New York: Doubleday, 1968.

1532 MASSON, Rosaline. *The Life of Robert Louis Stevenson*. Edinburgh: Chambers, 1923.

1533 SMITH, Janet Adam. *R. L. Stevenson*. London: Duckworth, 1937.*

1534 STRONG, Isobel, and Lloyd OSBORNE. *Memories of Vailima*. New York: Scribner, 1902.

Criticism

1535 BROWN, George E. *A Book of R. L. S.: Works, Travels, Friends, and Commentators.* New York: Scribner, 1919.

1536 BURRISS, Eli E. "The Classical Culture of Robert Louis Stevenson." *Classical Journal,* XX (1925), 271–279.

1537 CHESTERTON, G. K. *Robert Louis Stevenson.* New York: Dodd, 1928.*

1538 CLARK, Evert M. "The Kinship of Hazlitt and Stevenson." *University of Texas Studies in English,* IV (1924), 97–114.

1539 DAICHES, David. *Robert Louis Stevenson.* Norfolk, Conn.: New Directions, 1947.*

1540 DAICHES, David. *Robert Louis Stevenson and His World.* London: Thames and Hudson, 1973.

1541 EIGNER, Edwin M. *Robert Louis Stevenson and Romantic Tradition.* Princeton: Princeton University Press, 1966.

1542 GARROD, H. W. "The Poetry of R. L. Stevenson," *The Profession of Poetry and Other Lectures.* Oxford: Clarendon Press, 1929.

1543 HAMMERTON, J. A., ed. *Stevensoniana,* 2nd edition. Edinburgh: Grant, 1907.

1544 HENLEY, William Ernest. "R. L. S." *Pall Mall Magazine,* XXV (1901), 505–514.

1545 KELMAN, John, Jr. *The Faith of Robert Louis Stevenson.* Edinburgh: Oliphant Anderson Ferrier, 1903.

1546 KIELY, Robert. *Robert Louis Stevenson and the Fiction of Adventure.* Cambridge: Harvard University Press, 1964.*

1547 McKAY, George L., comp. *A Stevenson Library,* 6 vols. New Haven: Yale University Library, 1951–1964.

1548 McLAREN, M. D. S. *Stevenson and Edinburgh.* London: Chapman, 1950.

1549 MacLEAN, Cecil. *La France dans l'oeuvre de R. L. Stevenson.* Paris: Jouve, 1936.

1550 PRIDEAUX, W. F. *A Bibliography of the Works of Robert Louis Stevenson.* London: Hollings, 1917.

1551 RIEDEL, F. C. "A Classical Rhetorical Analysis of Some Elements of Stevenson's Essay Style." *Style,* III (1969), 182–199.

1552 ROBERTSON, Stuart. "Sir Thomas Browne and R. L. Stevenson." *Journal of English and Germanic Philology,* XX (1921), 371–384.

1553 SMITH, Janet Adam, ed. *Henry James and Robert Louis Stevenson.* New York: Macmillan, 1949.

1554 SNYDER, Alice D. "Paradox and Antithesis in Stevenson's Essays: A Structural Study." *Journal of English and Germanic Philology,* XIX (1920), 540–559.

1555 STEPHEN, Leslie. "The Style and Genius of Stevenson," *Studies of a Biographer,* 4 vols. New York: Putnam, 1907.

1556 VANDIVER, E. P., Jr. "Stevenson and Shakespeare." *Shakespeare Association Bulletin,* XIV (1939), 233–238.

Swinburne, Algernon Charles
(1837–1909)

Editions

1557 GOSSE, Edmund, and Thomas J. WISE, eds. *Complete Works,* Bonchurch Edition, 20 vols. New York: Wells, 1925–1927.*

1558 LANG, Cecil, ed. *The Swinburne Letters,* 6 vols. New Haven: Yale University Press, 1959–1962.*

1559 DOBRÉE, Bonamy, ed. *Poems of Algernon Charles Swinburne.* London: Penguin Books, 1961. [Penguin Poets, D-55.]

1560 HARE, Humphrey, ed. *Selected Poems.* London: Heinemann, 1950.

1561 HYDER, Clyde K., and Lewis CHASE, ed. *The Best of Swinburne.* New York: Nelson, 1937.

1562 SITWELL, Edith, ed. *Swinburne: A Selection.* London: Weidenfeld Nicolson, 1960.

1563 ROSENBERG, John D., ed. *Swinburne: Selected Poetry and Prose.* New York: Modern Library, 1968.

1564 HYDER, Clyde K., ed. *Swinburne as Critic.* London: Routledge Kegan Paul, 1972.

1565 HYDER, Clyde K., ed. *Swinburne Replies: Notes on Poems and Reviews, Under the Microscope, Dedicatory Epistle.* Syracuse, N.Y.: Syracuse University Press, 1966.

1566 WILSON, Edmund, ed. *The Novels of A. C. Swinburne: Love's Cross-Currents and Lesbia Brandon.* New York: Farrar Straus, 1963.

Biography

1567 BEERBOHM, Max. "No. 2, The Pines: Reminiscences of Swinburne," *And Even Now.* New York: Dutton, 1921.

1568 FULLER, Jean Overton. *Swinburne: A Critical Biography.* London: Chatto and Windus, 1968.

1569 GOSSE, Edmund. *The Life of Algernon Charles Swinburne.* New York: Macmillan, 1917. [Also as vol. XIX of *Complete Works,* See **1557.**]

1570 HARE, Humphrey. *Swinburne: A Biographical Approach.* London: Witherby, 1949.

1571 HENDERSON, Philip. *Swinburne: Portrait of a Poet.* New York: Macmillan, 1974.*

1572 KERNAHAN, Coulson. *Swinburne as I Knew Him.* London: Lane, 1919.

1573 LAFOURCADE, Georges. *La Jeunesse de Swinburne, 1837–1867,* 2 vols. London: Oxford University Press, 1928.

1574 LAFOURCADE, Georges. *Swinburne: A Literary Biography.* London: Bell, 1932.*

1575 LANG, Cecil. "Swinburne's Lost Love." *PMLA,* LXXIV (1959), 123–130.

1576 NICOLSON, Harold. *Swinburne.* London: Macmillan, 1926.

1577 PANTER-DOWNES, Mollie. *At the Pines.* London: Hamish Hamilton, 1971. [Swinburne's later life.]

1578 POUND, Ezra. "Swinburne versus Biographers." *Poetry,* XI (1918), 322–329.

1579 WATTS-DUNTON, Clara. *The Home Life of Swinburne.* London: Philpot, 1922.

1580 WOODBERRY, George E. *Swinburne.* New York: McClure, 1905.

Criticism

1581 ARVIN, Newton. "Swinburne as a Critic." *Sewanee Review,* XXXII (1924), 405–412.

1582 BROWN, E. K. "Swinburne: A Centenary Estimate." See **155.**

1583 BUCHANAN, Robert W. *The Fleshly School.* See **1415.**

1584 CASSIDY, John A. *Algernon C. Swinburne.* New York: Twayne, 1964.

1585 CHEW, Samuel C. *Swinburne.* Boston: Little Brown, 1929.

1586 CONNOLLY, T. E. "Swinburne on 'The Music of Poetry,' " *PMLA,* LXXII (1957), 680–688.

1587 COULLING, Sidney M. B. "Swinburne and Arnold." *Philological Quarterly.* XLIX (1970), 211–233.

1588 DRINKWATER, John. *Swinburne: An Estimate.* London: Dent, 1924.

1589 EHRSAM, T. G., *et al. Bibliographies.* See **72.**

1590 ELIOT, T. S. "Swinburne as Poet." *The Sacred Wood.* London: Methuen, 1920.*

1591 FINDLAY, Leonard M. "Swinburne and Tennyson." *Victorian Poetry,* IX (1971), 217–236.

1592 FISHER, Benjamin Franklin, IV. "Swinburne's *Tristram of Lyonesse* in Process." *Texas Studies in Literature and Language,* XIV (1972), 510–528.

1593 GRANVILLE-BARKER, Harley. "Some Victorians Afield: The Poet as Dramatist." See **1690.**

1594 HEARN, Lafcadio. "Studies in Swinburne," *Pre-Raphaelite and Other Poets.* New York: Dodd Mead, 1922.

1595 HYDER, Clyde K. "Algernon Charles Swinburne." See **81.**

1596 HYDER, Clyde K. *Swinburne's Literary Career and Fame.* Durham, N.C.: Duke University Press, 1933.*

1597 HYDER, Clyde K., ed. *Swinburne: The Critical Heritage.* London: Routledge Kegan Paul, 1970.

1598 LAFOURCADE, Georges. "Swinburne et Baudelaire." *Revue Anglo-Américaine,* II (1924), 183–196.

1599 LOUGY, Robert E. "Swinburne's Poetry and Twentieth-Century Criticism." *Dalhousie Review,* XLVIII (1968), 358–365.

1600 MACKAIL, John W. "Swinburne," *Studies of English Poets.* See **1213.**

1601 McGANN, Jerome J. *Swinburne: An Experiment in Criticism.* Chicago: University of Chicago Press, 1972.

1602 McGHEE, Richard D. " 'Thalassius': Swinburne's Poetic Myth." *Victorian Poetry,* V (1967), 127–136.

1603 McSWEENEY, Kerry. "The Structure of Swinburne's 'Tristram of Lyonesse.' " *Queen's Quarterly,* XXV (1968), 690–702.

1604 MEYNELL, Alice. "Swinburne's Lyrical Poetry," *Hearts of Controversy.* London: Burns, 1918.

1605 PACKER, Lona Mosk. "Swinburne and Christina Rossetti: Atheist and Anglican." *University of Toronto Quarterly,* XXXIII (1963), 30–42.

1606 PETERS, Robert L. *The Crowns of Apollo: Swinburne's Principles of Literature and Art.* Detroit: Wayne State University Press, 1965.*

1607 RATCHFORD, Fannie E. "Swinburne at Work." *Sewanee Review,* XXXI (1923), 353–362.

1608 RAYMOND, Meredith B. *Swinburne's Poetics: Theory and Practice.* The Hague: Mouton, 1971.*

1609 REED, John R. "Swinburne's *Tristram of Lyonesse:* The Poet-Lover's Song of Love." *Victorian Poetry,* IV (1966), 99–120.

1610 RIDENOUR, George M. "Swinburne on 'The Problem to Solve in Expression.' " *Victorian Poetry,* IX (1971), 129–144.

1611 ROSENBERG, John D. "Swinburne." *Victorian Studies,* XI (1967), 131–152. [Also as introduction to **1563**.]

1612 RUTLAND, William R. *Swinburne: A Nineteenth-Century Hellene.* Oxford: Blackwell, 1931.

1613 SAINTSBURY, George. "Mr. Swinburne," *Corrected Impressions.* New York: Dodd Mead, 1895.

1614 SQUIRE, J. C. "Swinburne's Defects," *Books in General,* Third Series. London: Heinemann, 1921.

1615 SYMONS, Arthur. "Swinburne," *Studies in Strange Souls.* London: Sawyer, 1929.

1616 WELBY, T. Earle. *A Study of Swinburne.* New York: Doran, 1926.*

1617 WIER, Marion C. *The Influence of Aeschylus and Euripides on the Structure and Content of Swinburne's "Atalanta in Calydon" and "Erechtheus."* Ann Arbor, Mich.: Wahr, 1920.

1618 WISE, Thomas J. *A Bibliography of the Writings in Prose and Verse of Algernon Charles Swinburne,* 2 vols. London: Clay, 1919–1920. [Also issued as vol. XX of *Complete Works;* not entirely reliable—lists several of Wise's forgeries.]

Tennyson, Alfred, Lord (1809–1892)

Editions

1619 TENNYSON, Hallam, Lord., ed. *Works,* 6 vols. New York: Macmillan, 1908.

1620 ROLFE, W. J., ed. *The Poetic and Dramatic Works.* Boston: Houghton Mifflin, 1898.

1621 TENNYSON, Sir Charles, ed. *The Devil and the Lady and Unpublished Early Poems.* Bloomington: Indiana University Press, 1964.

1622 AUDEN, W. H., ed. *A Selection from the Poems.* Garden City, N.Y.: Doubleday, 1944.

1623 BUCKLEY, Jerome H., ed. *Poems of Tennyson*. Boston: Houghton Mifflin, 1958. [Riverside Editions, B26.]

1624 BUSH, Douglas, ed. *Selected Poetry*. New York: Modern Library, 1951. [MLCE, T60.]

1625 RICKS, Christopher, ed. *The Poems of Tennyson*. London: Longmans, 1969.*

1626 SOUTHAM, B. C., ed. *Lord Tennyson: Selected Poems*. London: Chatto and Windus, 1964.

1627 PFORDRESHER, John, ed. *A Variorum Edition of Tennyson's Idylls of the King*. New York: Columbia University Press, 1973.

1628 ROSS, Robert H., ed. *In Memoriam*. New York: Norton, 1973. [Norton Critical Edition paperback.]

1629 HILL, Robert W., Jr., ed. *Tennyson's Poetry*. New York: Norton, 1971. [Norton Critical Edition paperback.]

1630 DYSON, Hope, and Sir Charles TENNYSON, eds. *Dear and Honoured Lady*. London: Macmillan, 1970. [Correspondence between Tennyson and Queen Victoria.]

Biography

1631 BROOKFIELD, Frances A. *The Cambridge Apostles*. New York: Scribner, 1906.

1632 FAUSSET, Hugh I'A. *Tennyson: A Modern Portrait*. London: Selwyn, 1923.

1633 LOUNSBURY, T. R. *The Life and Times of Tennyson*. New Haven: Yale University Press, 1915.

1634 MILLER, Betty. "Tennyson: The Early Years." *Twentieth Century*, CLXVII (1960), 520–529.

1635 NICOLSON, Sir Harold. *Tennyson: Aspects of His Life, Character, and Poetry*. London: Constable, 1949.

1636 RADER, Ralph W. *Tennyson's "Maud": The Biographical Genesis*. Berkeley: University of California Press, 1963.*

1637 RAWNSLEY, H. D. *Memories of the Tennysons*. Glasgow: MacLehose, 1900.

1638 RICHARDSON, Joanna. *The Pre-eminent Victorian: A Study of Tennyson*. London: Cape, 1962.

1639 RITCHIE, Anne Thackeray. *Records of Tennyson, Ruskin, and the Brownings*. New York: Harper, 1892.

1640 TENNYSON, Sir Charles. *Alfred Tennyson*. New York: Macmillan, 1949.*

1641 TENNYSON, Sir Charles. "The Somersby Tennysons." *Victorian Studies*, Christmas Supplement, 1963.

1642 TENNYSON, Hallam, Lord. *Alfred, Lord Tennyson: A Memoir*, 2 vols. New York: Macmillan, 1897.*

1643 TENNYSON, Hallam, Lord. *Tennyson and His Friends*. London: Macmillan, 1911.

Criticism

1644 ALAYA, Flavia M. "Tennyson's 'The Lady of Shalott': The Triumph of Art." *Victorian Poetry,* VIII (1971), 273–290.

1645 ANTIPPAS, Andy P. "Tennyson's Sinful Soul: Poetic Tradition and 'Keats Turned Imbecile.' " *Tulane Studies in English,* XVII (1969), 113–134. [On "The Palace of Art."]

1646 ASSAD, Thomas J. "Analogy in Tennyson's 'Crossing the Bar.' " *Tulane Studies in English,* VIII (1958), 153–164.

1647 ASSAD, Thomas J. "On the Major Poems of Tennyson's *Enoch Arden* Volume." *Tulane Studies in English,* XIV (1965), 29–56.

1648 ASSAD, Thomas J. "Tennyson's 'Break, Break, Break.' " *Tulane Studies in English,* XII (1963), 71–80.

1649 ASSAD, Thomas J. "Tennyson's 'Tears, Idle Tears.' " *Tulane Studies in English,* XIII (1963), 71–83.

1650 ASSAD, Thomas J. "Tennyson's Use of the Tripartite View of Man in Three Songs from *The Princess.*" *Tulane Studies in English,* XV (1967), 31–58.

1651 AUGUST, Eugene R. "Tennyson and Teilhard: The Faith of *In Memoriam.*" *PMLA,* LXXXIV (1969), 217–226.

1652 BAGEHOT, Walter. "Wordsworth, Tennyson, and Browning," *Literary Studies,* 3 vols. London: Longmans, 1895.

1653 BAKER, A. E. *A Concordance to the Poetical and Dramatic Works of Alfred, Lord Tennyson.* New York: Macmillan, 1914. [Reprinted, New York: Barnes and Noble, 1966.]

1654 BAKER, A. E. *A Tennyson Dictionary.* New York: Dutton, 1916.

1655 BALL, Patricia M. "Tennyson and the Romantics." *Victorian Poetry,* I (1963), 7–16.

1656 BAUM, Paull F. *Tennyson Sixty Years After.* Chapel Hill: University of North Carolina Press, 1948.

1657 BENTON, R. P. "Tennyson and Lao Tzu." *Philosophy East and West,* XII (1962), 233–240.

1658 BISHOP, Jonathan. "The Unity of *In Memoriam.*" *Victorian Newsletter,* #21 (1962), 9–14.

1659 BOAS, F. S. *"The Idylls of the King* in 1921." *Nineteenth Century,* XC (1921), 819–830.

1660 BOWDEN, Marjorie. *Tennyson in France.* Manchester: Manchester University Press, 1930.

1661 BRADLEY, A. C. *A Commentary on Tennyson's 'In Memoriam.'* London: Macmillan, 1930.*

1662 BRADLEY, A. C. "The Reaction against Tennyson," *A Miscellany.* London: Macmillan, 1929.

1663 BRASHEAR, William B. *The Living Will: A Study of Tennyson and Nineteenth-Century Subjectivism.* The Hague: Mouton, 1969.*

1664 BROOKE, Stopford A. *Tennyson: His Art and Relation to Modern Life,* 2 vols. London: Isbister, 1900.

ALFRED, LORD TENNYSON

1665 BUCKLEY, Jerome H. *Tennyson: The Growth of a Poet*. Cambridge: Harvard University Press, 1960.*

1666 BUCKLEY, Jerome H. "Tennyson's Irony." *Victorian Newsletter*, #31 (Spring, 1967), 7–10.

1667 BUFKIN, E. C. "Imagery in 'Locksley Hall.' " *Victorian Poetry*, II (1964), 21–28.

1668 BUSH, Douglas. *Mythology and the Romantic Tradition*. See **55**.

1669 CADBURY, William. "Tennyson's 'The Palace of Art' and the Rhetoric of Structures." *Criticism*, VII (1965), 23–44.

1670 CAMPBELL, Nancie, ed. *Tennyson in Lincoln: A Catalogue of the Collections in the Research Centre*, 2 vols. Lincoln, England: Tennyson Research Centre, 1971, 1973.

1671 CARR, Arthur J. "Tennyson as a Modern Poet." *University of Toronto Quarterly*, XIX (1950), 361–382.

1672 COLLINS, J. C. *Illustrations of Tennyson*. London: Chatto, 1891.

1673 COLLINS, Winston. *"The Princess:* The Education of the Prince." *Victorian Poetry*, XI (1973), 285–294.

1674 DAHL, Curtis. "A Double Frame for Tennyson's Demeter?" *Victorian Studies*, I (1958), 356–362.

1675 DANZIG, Allan. "The Contraries: A Central Concept in Tennyson's Poetry." *PMLA*, LXXVII (1962), 577–585.

1676 DANZIG, Allan. "Tennyson's *The Princess:* A Definition of Love." *Victorian Poetry*, IV (1966), 83–89.

1677 DE MOTT, Benjamin. "The General, the Poet, and the Inquisition." *Kenyon Review*, XXIV (1962), 442–456. [On "The Lotos-Eaters".]

1678 DOWDEN, Edward. "Mr. Tennyson and Mr. Browning," *Studies in Literature*, London: Paul, 1882.

1679 DUNCAN, Edgar Hill. "Tennyson: A Modern Appraisal." *Tennessee Studies in Literature*, IV (1959), 13–30.

1680 EGGERS, J. Philip. *King Arthur's Laureate: A Study of Tennyson's Idylls of the King*. New York: New York University Press, 1971.*

1681 EHRSAM, T. G., *et al. Bibliographies*. See **72**.

1682 EIDSON, J. O. *Tennyson in America*. Athens: University of Georgia Press, 1943.

1683 ELIOT, T. S. "In Memoriam," *Essays, Ancient and Modern*. New York: Harcourt Brace, 1936.*

1684 ELTON, Oliver. *Alfred Tennyson and Matthew Arnold*. London: Arnold, 1924.

1685 FICHTER, Andrew. "Ode and Elegy: Idea and Form in Tennyson's Early Poetry." *English Literary History*, XL (1973), 398–427.

1686 FREDEMAN, William E. "The Sphere of Common Duties: The Domestic Solution in Tennyson's Poetry." *Bulletin of John Rylands Library*, LIV (1972), 356–383.

1687 FULWEILER, Howard W. "Tennyson and the 'Summons from the Sea.' " *Victorian Poetry*, III (1965), 25–44.

1688 GENUNG, J. F. *Tennyson's "In Memoriam": Its Purpose and Its Structure*. Boston: Houghton Mifflin, 1884.

1689 GORDON, W. C. *The Social Ideals of Alfred Tennyson as Related to His Time*. Chicago: University of Chicago Press, 1906.

ALFRED, LORD TENNYSON

1690 GRANVILLE-BARKER, Harley. "Some Victorians Afield: The Poet as Dramatist." *Fortnightly Review,* CXXXI (1929), 655–672. Also in **87.**

1691 GRAY, J. M. *Man and Myth in Victorian England: Tennyson's "The Coming of Arthur."* Lincoln, England: The Tennyson Society, 1969.

1692 GRAY, J. M. *Tennyson's Doppelgänger: Balin and Balan.* Lincoln, England: The Tennyson Society, 1971.

1693 GROB, Alan. "Tennyson's 'The Lotos-Eaters': Two Versions of Art." *Modern Philology,* LXII (1964), 118–129.

1694 GROOM, Bernard. *On the Diction of Tennyson, Browning and Arnold.* New York: Oxford University Press, 1939.

1695 GWYNN, Stephen. *Tennyson: A Critical Study.* London: Blackie, 1899.

1696 HAIGHT, Gordon S. "Tennyson's Merlin." *Studies in Philology,* XLIV (1947), 549–566.

1697 HALLAM, Arthur Henry. "On Some Characteristics of Modern Poetry and on the Lyrical Poems of Alfred Tennyson," *Literary Remains.* Boston: Tickner, 1863.

1698 HELLSTROM, Ward. *On the Poems of Tennyson.* Gainesville: University of Florida Press, 1972.

1699 HUNT, John Dixon. "The Poetry of Distance: Tennyson's *Idylls of the King."* See **49.**

1700 HUNT, John Dixon. "The Symbolist Vision of *In Memoriam."* *Victorian Poetry,* VII (1970), 187–198.

1701 HUTTON, Richard Holt. "Tennyson," *Literary Essays.* London: Macmillan, 1892.

1702 JAMES, Henry. "Tennyson's Drama: *Queen Mary* and *Harold,"* *Views and Reviews.* Boston: Ball, 1908.

1703 JAPIKSE, Cornelia G. *The Dramas of Alfred, Lord Tennyson.* London: Macmillan, 1926.

1704 JOHNSON, E. D. H. *The Alien Visions.* See **98.**

1705 JOHNSON, E. D. H. *"In Memoriam:* The Way of the Poet." *Victorian Studies,* II (1958), 139–148.

1706 JOHNSON, E. D. H. "Tennyson." See **81.**

1707 JOHNSON, E. D. H. "The Lily and the Rose: Symbolic Meaning in Tennyson's *Maud."* *PMLA,* LXIV (1949), 1222–1227.

1708 JONES, Richard, *The Growth of "The Idylls of the King."* Philadelphia: Lippincott, 1895.

1709 JOSEPH, Gerhard J. "Poe and Tennyson." *PMLA,* LXXXVIII (1973), 418–428.

1710 JOSEPH, Gerhard J. *Tennysonian Love: The Strange Diagonal.* Minneapolis: University of Minnesota Press, 1969.*

1711 JUMP, J. D., ed. *Tennyson: The Critical Heritage.* London: Routledge Kegan Paul, 1967.

1712 KAPLAN, Fred. "Woven Paces and Waving Hands: Tennyson's Merlin as Fallen Artist." *Victorian Poetry,* VII (1969), 285–298.

1713 KILLHAM, John, ed. *Critical Essays on the Poetry of Tennyson.* London: Routledge Kegan Paul, 1960.

1714 KILLHAM, John. *Tennyson and "The Princess": Reflections of an Age.* London: Athlone Press, 1958.

1715 KISSANE, James D. *Alfred Tennyson.* New York: Twayne, 1970.

ALFRED, LORD TENNYSON

1716 KISSANE, James D. "Tennyson: The Passion of the Past and the Curse of Time." *ELM*, XXXII (1965), 85–109.

1717 KOZICKI, Henry. "Tennyson's *Idylls of the King* as Tragic Drama." *Victorian Poetry*, IV (1966), 15–20.

1718 LAYARD, G. S. *Tennyson and His Pre-Raphaelite Illustrators*. London: Stock, 1894.

1719 LITZINGER, Boyd. "The Structure of Tennyson's 'The Last Tournament.' " *Victorian Poetry*, I (1963), 53–60.

1720 LOCKYER, Sir Norman and W. L. LOCKYER. *Tennyson as a Student of Science*. London: Macmillan, 1910.

1721 MARSHALL, George O. *A Tennyson Handbook*. New York: Twayne, 1964.

1722 MASTERMAN, C. F. G. *Tennyson as a Religious Teacher*. London: Methuen, 1900.

1723 MATTES, Eleanor B. *In Memoriam: The Way of a Soul*. New York: Exposition Press, 1951.

1724 MAYNADIER, G. H. *The Arthur of the English Poets*. Boston: Houghton Mifflin, 1907.

1725 MAYS, J. C. C. "*In Memoriam:* An Aspect of Form." *University of Toronto Quarterly*, XXXV (1965), 22–46.

1726 MERMIN, Dorothy M. "Tennyson's *Maud:* A Thematic Analysis." *Texas Studies in Literature and Language*, XV (1973), 267–277.

1727 METZGER, Lore. "The Eternal Process: Parallels between Goethe's *Faust* and *In Memoriam*." *Victorian Poetry*, I (1963), 189–196.

1728 MILLER, Betty. "Tennyson and the Sinful Queen." *Twentieth Century*, CLVIII (1955), 355–363.

1729 MILLHAUSER, Milton. *Fire and Ice: The Influence of Science on Tennyson's Poetry*. Lincoln, England: The Tennyson Society, 1971.

1730 MITCHELL, Charles. "The Undying Will of Tennyson's Ulysses." *Victorian Poetry*, II (1964), 87–95.

1731 MOORE, Carlisle. "Faith, Doubt, and Mystical Experience in *In Memoriam*." *Victorian Studies*, VII (1963), 155–169.

1732 MUSTARD, W. P. *Classical Echoes in Tennyson*. New York: Macmillan, 1904.

1733 MYERS, F. W. H. "Tennyson as a Prophet," *Science and a Future Life*. London: Macmillan, 1893.

1734 OSTRIKER, Alicia. "The Three Modes in Tennyson's Prosody." *PMLA*, LXXXII (1967), 273–284.

1735 PACKER, Lona Mosk. "Sun and Shadow: The Nature of Experience in Tennyson's 'The Lady of Shalott.' " *Victorian Newsletter*, #25 (1964), 4–8.

1736 PADEN, W. D. *Tennyson in Egypt*. Lawrence: University of Kansas Press, 1942. [On the imagery of the early poems.]

1737 PALMER, D. J., ed. *Alfred Tennyson*. London: Bell, 1973. [Also Ohio University paperback. A collection of modern critical essays.]*

1738 PITT, Valerie. *Tennyson Laureate*. London: Barrie and Rockliff, 1962.

1739 PREYER, Robert O. "Alfred Tennyson: The Poetry and Politics of Conservative Vision." *Victorian Studies*, IX (1966), 325–352.

1740 PREYER, Robert O. "Tennyson as an Oracular Poet." *Modern Philology*, LV (1958), 239–251.

ALFRED, LORD TENNYSON

1741 PRIESTLEY, F. E. L. *Language and Structure in Tennyson's Poetry*. London: Deutsch, 1973.

1742 PRIESTLEY, F. E. L. "Locksley Hall Revisited." *Queen's Quarterly*, XXXI (1974), 512–531.

1743 PRIESTLEY, F. E. L. "Tennyson's Idylls." *University of Toronto Quarterly*, XIX (1949), 35–49.*

1744 PYRE, J. F. A. *The Formation of Tennyson's Style*. Madison: University of Wisconsin Press, 1921.

1745 RAY, Gordon. "Tennyson Reads *Maud*." W. Paul Elledge and Richard L. Hoffman, eds., *Romantic and Victorian: Studies in Memory of William H. Marshall*. Rutherford, N.J.: Fairleigh Dickinson University Press, 1971.

1746 REED, John R. "The Design of Tennyson's 'The Two Voices.' " *University of Toronto Quarterly*, XXXVII (1968), 186–196.

1747 REED, John R. *Perception and Design in Tennyson's Idylls of the King*. Athens: Ohio University Press, 1971.*

1748 RICKS, Christopher. *Tennyson*. New York: Macmillan, 1972.*

1749 ROBINSON, Edna. *Tennyson's Use of the Bible*. Baltimore: Furst, 1917.

1750 ROPPEN, Georg. " 'Ulysses' and Tennyson's Sea-Quest." *English Studies*, XL (1959), 77–90.

1751 ROSENBERG, John D. *The Fall of Camelot: A Study of Tennyson's Idylls of the King*. Cambridge: Harvard University Press, 1973.*

1752 ROSENBERG, John D. "The Two Kingdoms of *In Memoriam*." *Journal of English and Germanic Philology*, VIII (1959), 228–240.

1753 ROYCE, Josiah. "Tennyson and Pessimism," *Studies of Good and Evil*. New York: Appleton, 1898.

1754 RYALS, Clyde de L. *From the Great Deep: Essays on Idylls of the King*. Athens: Ohio University Press, 1967.

1755 RYALS, Clyde de L. *Theme and Symbol in Tennyson's Poems to 1850*. Philadelphia: University of Pennsylvania Press, 1964.*

1756 SALT, H. S. *Tennyson as a Thinker*, London: Fifield, 1909.

1757 SANDERS, Charles R. "Carlyle and Tennyson." *PMLA*, LXXVI (1961), 82–97.

1758 SCAIFE, C. H. O. *The Poetry of Alfred Tennyson*. London: Cobden-Sanderson, 1930.

1759 SCOTT, P. G. *Tennyson's "Enoch Arden": A Victorian Bestseller*. Lincoln, England: The Tennyson Society, 1970.

1760 SENDRY, Joseph. *"In Memoriam* and *Lycidas*." *PMLA*, LXXXII (1967), 437–443.

1761 SENDRY, Joseph. " 'The Palace of Art' Revisited." *Victorian Poetry*, IV (1966), 149–162.

1762 SHANNON, Edgar F., Jr. *Tennyson and the Reviewers*. Cambridge: Harvard University Press, 1952.

1763 SHAW, W. David. "The Idealist's Dilemma in *Idylls of the King*." *Victorian Poetry*, V (1967), 41–53.

1764 SHAW, W. David. " *In Memoriam* and the Rhetoric of Confession." *English Literary History*, XXXVIII (1972), 80–103.

1765 SIMPSON Arthur L., Jr. "Aurora as Artist: A Reinterpretation of Tennyson's *Tithonus*." *Philological Quarterly*, LI (1971), 905–921.

ALFRED, LORD TENNYSON

1766 SINFIELD, Alan. *The Language of Tennyson's In Memoriam*. New York: Barnes and Noble, 1971.

1767 SMALLEY, Donald. "A New Look at Tennyson, and Especially the *Idylls*." *Journal of English and Germanic Philology*, LXI (1962), 349–357.

1768 SMITH, Elton F. *The Two Voices: A Tennyson Study*. Lincoln: University of Nebraska Press, 1964.

1769 SNEATH, E. H. *The Mind of Tennyson*. New York: Scribner, 1900.

1770 SOLOMON, Stanley J. "Tennyson's Paradoxical King." *Victorian Poetry*, I (1963), 258–271.

1771 SOUTHAM, B. C. *Tennyson*. London: Longmans, 1971. [British Council pamphlet.]

1772 STAINES, David. "The Prose Drafts of Tennyson's *Idylls of the King*." *Harvard Library Bulletin*, XXII (1974), 280–308.

1773 STAINES, David. "Tennyson's 'The Holy Grail': The Tragedy of Percivale." *Modern Language Review*, LXIX (1974), 745–756.

1774 STANGE, G. R. "Tennyson's Garden of Art: A Study of 'The Hesperides.' " *PMLA*, LXVII (1952), 732–743.

1775 STARNES, D. W. T. "The Influence of Carlyle upon Tennyson." *Texas Review*, VI (1921), 316–336.

1776 STEANE, J. B. *Tennyson*. London: Evans, 1966.

1777 STOKES, Edward. "The Metrics of *Maud*." *Victorian Poetry*, II (1964), 97–110.

1778 SVAGLIC, Martin J. "A Framework for Tennyson's *In Memoriam*." *Journal of English and Germanic Philology*, LXI (1962), 810–825.

1779 SWINBURNE, A. C. *Under the Microscope*. London: White, 1872. [Attack on *Idylls of the King*.]

1780 TENNYSON, Sir Charles, and Christine FALL, eds. *Alfred Tennyson: An Annotated Bibliography*. Athens: University of Georgia Press, 1967.

1781 TENNYSON, Sir Charles. "The Dream in Tennyson's Poetry." *Virginia Quarterly Review*, XL (1964), 228–248.

1782 TENNYSON, Sir Charles. "The Idylls of the King." *Twentieth Century*, CLXI (1957), 277–286.

1783 TENNYSON, Sir Charles. *Six Tennyson Essays*. London: Cassell, 1954.*

1784 TILLOTSON, Geoffrey, and Kathleen TILLOTSON. *Mid-Victorian Studies*. London: Athlone Press, 1965. [Contains essay on the *Idylls*.]

1785 TURNER, Paul. "Some Ancient Light on Tennyson's *Oenone*." *Journal of English and Germanic Philology*, LXI (1962), 52–72.

1786 WEATHERHEAD, L. D. "Tennyson's Afterworld." *London Quarterly Review*. CXLIV (1925), 157–174.

1787 WHITING, George W. "The Artist and Tennyson." *Rice University Studies in Literature*, L (1964), 1–84.

1788 WHITMAN, Walt. "A Word about Tennyson." *November Boughs*. Philadelphia: McKay, 1888.

1789 WILKENFELD, R. B. "The Shape of Two Voices." *Victorian Poetry*, IV (1966), 163–173.

1790 WILKENFELD, R. B. "Tennyson's Camelot: The Kingdom of Folly." *University of Toronto Quarterly*, XXXVII (1968), 281–294.

Thomson, James
(1834–1882)

Editions

1791 DOBELL, Bertram, ed. *Poetical Works*, 2 vols. London: Reeves, 1895.

1792 GEROULD, G. H., ed. *Poems*. New York: Holt, 1927

1793 RIDLER, Anne, ed. *Poems and Some Letters*. London: Centaur Press, 1963.

1794 ROBERTSON, J. M., ed. *Poems, Essays, and Fragments*. London: Fifield, 1905.

1795 SCHAEFER, William D., ed. *The Speedy Extinction of Evil and Misery: Selected Prose of James Thomson*. Berkeley: University of California Press, 1967.

Biography and Criticism

1796 BYRON, Kenneth H. *The Pessimism of James Thomson (B.V.) in Relation to his Times*. The Hague: Mouton, 1965.

1797 DOBELL, Bertram. *The Laureate of Pessimism*. London: Dobell, 1910.

1798 FORSYTH, R. A. "Evolutionism and the Pessimism of James Thomson (B.V.)." *Essays in Criticism*, XII (1962), 148–166.

1799 HARPER, George M. "Blake's *Nebuchadnezzar* in 'The City of Dreadful Night.' " *Studies in Philology*, L (1953), 68–70.

1800 HEARN, Lafcadio. "Pessimists and Their Kindred," *Interpretations*. See **702.**

1801 HOFFMAN, H. "An Angel in the City of Dreadful Night." *Sewanee Review,* XXXII (1924), 317–335.

1802 LE ROY, Gaylord C. "James Thomson." *Perplexed Prophets*. Philadelphia: University of Pennsylvania Press, 1953.

1803 McGANN, Jerome J. "James Thomson (B.V.); The Woven Hymns of Night and Day." *Studies in English Literature*, III (1963), 493–507.

1804 MARKS, Jeannette. "Disaster and Poetry: A Study of James Thomson." *North American Review*, CCXII (1920), 93–109.

1805 PEYRE, Henri. "Les Sources du pessimisme de Thomson." *Revue Anglo-Américaine*, 1924, pp. 152–156; 1925, pp. 217–231.

1806 SALT, Henry S. *The Life of James Thomson*. London: Watts, 1914.

1807 SCHAEFER, William D. "The Two Cities of Dreadful Night." *PMLA,* LXXVII (1962), 609–615.

1808 SCHAEFER, William D. *James Thomson (B.V.): Beyond "The City."* Berkeley: University of California Press, 1965.*

1809 SYMONS, Arthur. "James Thomson," *Studies in Two Literature*. See **1354.**

1810 VACHOT, Charles. *James Thomson*. Paris: Didier, 1964.*

1811 WALKER, Imogene B. *James Thomson (B.V.): A Critical Study*. Ithaca, N.Y.: Cornell University Press, 1950.*

1812 ZABEL, Morton D. "James Thomson's Poems," *Poetry*, XXXII (1928), 229–233.

Wilde, Oscar
(1854 –1900)

Editions

1813 ROSS, Robert, ed. *Complete Works*, 10 vols. New York: Bigelow, 1921.

1814 ALDINGTON, Richard, ed. *The Portable Oscar Wilde*. New York: Viking, 1946.

1815 HOLLAND, Vyvyan, ed. *De Profundis*. New York: Philosophical Library, 1950.

1816 HART-DAVIS, Rupert, ed. *The Letters of Oscar Wilde*. London: Hart-Davis, 1962.*

1817 HOLLAND, Vyvyan, ed. *The Complete Works of Oscar Wilde*. London: Collins, 1966.

1818 ELLMANN, Richard, ed. *The Artist as Critic: Critical Writings of Oscar Wilde*. New York: Random House, 1968.*

1819 WEINTRAUB, Stanley, ed. *Literary Criticism of Oscar Wilde*. Lincoln: University of Nebraska Press, 1969. [Bison Books.]

Biography

1820 BRASOL, B. L. *Oscar Wilde, the Man, the Artist, the Martyr*. New York: Scribner, 1938.

1821 CROFT-COOKE, Rupert. *The Unrecorded Life of Oscar Wilde*. New York: McKay, 1972.*

1822 DOUGLAS, Lord Alfred. *Oscar Wilde: A Summing Up*. London: Richards, 1950.

1823 GIDE, André. *Oscar Wilde*. London: Kimber, 1951.

1824 HARRIS, Frank. Oscar Wilde: His Life and Confessions, ed. by Lyle Blair. East Lansing: Michigan State University Press, 1959.

1825 HOLLAND, Vyvyan. *Oscar Wilde: A Pictorial Biography*. London: Thames and Hudson, 1960.

1826 HOLLAND, Vyvyan. *Son of Oscar Wilde*. New York: Dutton, 1954.*

1827 HYDE, H. Montgomery. *Oscar Wilde: The Aftermath*. London: Methuen, 1963.

1828 HYDE, H. Montgomery. *Trials of Oscar Wilde*. Harmondsworth: Penguin Books, 1963.

1829 O'SULLIVAN, Vincent. *Aspects of Wilde*. New York: Holt, 1936.

1830 PEARSON, Hesketh. *The Life of Oscar Wilde*. London: Methuen, 1951.

1831 RENIER, G. J., *Oscar Wilde*. New York: Appleton, 1933.

1832 SHERARD, R. H. *The Life of Oscar Wilde*. New York: Dodd, 1928.

1833 WHITE, Terence de Vere. *The parents of Oscar Wilde: Sir William and Lady Wilde*. London: Hodder and Stoughton, 1967.

1834 WILSON, T. G. *Victorian Doctor: Being the Life of Sir William Wilde*. New York: Fischer, 1946.

1835 WYNDHAM, Horance. *Speranza: A Biography of Lady Wilde*. New York: Philosophical Library, 1952.

Criticism

1836 AGATE, J. E. *Oscar Wilde and the Theatre*. London: Curtain Press, 1947.

1837 BECKSON, Karl E., ed. *Oscar Wilde: The Critical Heritage*. London: Routledge Kegan Paul, 1970.

1838 BUTWIN, Joseph. "The Martyred Clown: Oscar Wilde in *De Profundis*." *Victorian Newsletter*, #42 (Fall, 1972), 1–6.

1839 ELLMAN, Richard, ed. *Oscar Wilde: A Collection of Critical Essays*. Englewood Cliffs, N.J.: Prentice Hall, 1969.

1840 FEHR, Bernhard. *Studien zu Oscar Wildes Gedichten*. Berlin: Mayer, 1922.

1841 FIDO, Martin. *Oscar Wilde*. New York: Viking, 1973. [A pictorial record.]

1842 GLAENZER, R. B., "The Story of the *Ballad of Reading Gaol*." *Bookman*, XXXIII (1911), 376–381.

1843 GORDON, Jan B. "Wilde and Newman: The Confessional Mode." *Renascence*, XXII (1970), 183–191.

1844 HARDWICK, Michael. *The Drake Guide to Oscar Wilde*. New York: Drake, 1973.

1845 JACKSON, Holbrook. "Oscar Wilde: The Last Phase," *The Eighteen Nineties. See* **97.**

1846 JULLIAN, Philippe. *Oscar Wilde*. New York: Viking, 1969.

1847 LE ROY, Gaylord C. "Oscar Wilde," *Perplexed Prophets*. See **1802.**

1848 MASON, Stuart. *Bibliography of Oscar Wilde*. London: Laurie, 1914. [Reprinted 1967.]

1849 NASSAAR, Christopher S. *Into the Demon Universe: A Literary Exploration of Oscar Wilde*. New Haven: Yale University Press, 1974.*

1850 OJALA, Aatos. *Aestheticism and Oscar Wilde*. Helsinki: Finnish Academy of Science and Letters, 1957.

1851 POAGUE, L. A. *"The Importance of Being Earnest:* The Texture of Wilde's Irony." *Modern Drama*, XVI (1973), 251–257.

1852 RODITI, Edouard. *Oscar Wilde*. Norfolk, Conn.: New Directions, 1947.*

1853 SAN JUAN, Epifanio, Jr. *The Art of Oscar Wilde*. Princeton: Princeton University Press, 1967.*

1854 SHANKS, Edward. "Oscar Wilde," *Second Essays on Literature*. London: Collins, 1927.

1855 SYMONS, Arthur. "An Artist in Attitudes: Oscar Wilde," *Studies in Prose and Verse*. London: Dent, 1904.

1856 THOMAS, J. D. " 'The Soul of Man under Socialism': An Essay in Context." *Rice University Studies*, LI (1965), 83–95.

1857 WILLOUGHBY, Leonard A. "Oscar Wilde and Goethe: The Life of Art and the Art of Life." *Publications of the English Goethe Society*, XXXV (1964), 1–37.

1858 WOODCOCK, George. *The Paradox of Oscar Wilde*. New York: Macmillan, 1950.*

INDEX

Consult the table of contents for major sections on individual Victorian poets and prose writers.

INDEX

INDEX

INDEX

INDEX

Grierson, H. J. C., 88, 514
Griffin, W. H., 355
Grob, Alan, 1693
Groom, Bernard, 253, 406, 1694
Gross, John, 89, 1018
Grylls, R. G., 1402
Guerard, A. J., 781, 782
Gwynn, Stephen, 1695

Haber, T. B., 925, 934, 935, 936
Haight, G. S., 690, 1107, 1696
Hair, Donald, 407
Halévy, Elie, 16
Hall, R. A., 733
Hallam, A. H., 1697
Hallam, J. H. 808
Halliday, R. J., 643
Hamburger, Joseph, 1146
Hamilton, Robert, 937
Hamilton, Walter, 1428
Hammerton, J. A., 1089, 1543
Hanley, E. A., 254
Hanson, E. M., 493
Hanson, L., 493
Harding, F. J. W., 255
Hardy, Barbara, 609
Hardy, Evelyn, 757, 761, 762
Hardy, F. E., 763
Hardwick, Michael, 1844
Hare, Humphrey, 1560, 1570
Harper, G. M., 1799
Harper, J. W., 408
Harris, Frank, 1824
Harris, W. V., 610, 1313, 1429
Harrison, Brian, 17
Harrison, Frederic, 1147, 1481
Harrison, J. F. E., 18
Harrison, T. P., 883
Harrold, C. F., 164, 515, 1238, 1239, 1240, 1274
Harrold, W. E., 409
Hart, J. D., 1526
Hart-Davis, Rupert, 1816
Hartman, G. H., 884
Harvey, C. H., 256
Hatcher, H. H., 410
Hawkins, Desmond, 783
Hawkins, Maude, 938
Hayek, F. A., 1131, 1148
Hayter, Alethea, 328
Hayward, John, 165
Hearn, Lafcadio, 90, 702, 1594, 1800
Hellstrom, Ward, 1698
Helyar, James, 734
Henderson, Philip, 1177, 1184, 1571
Henley, W. E., 1108, 1544
Henn, T. R., 1019
Henshaw, N. W., 735
Herbert, R. L., 1471

Herford, C. H., 1206
Hermann, E. A., 411
Heron-Allen, Edward, 703
Herrmann, Luke, 1501
Hesse, Eva, 391
Heuser, Alan, 885
Hewlett, Dorothy, 317
Heydon, P. N., 313
Hicks, Granville, 91
Hickson, C., 784
Hill, R. W., 1629
Hilton, Timothy, 92
Himmelfarb, Gertrude, 644, 1149
Hind, C. L., 838
Hoare, D. M., 1207
Hoctor, Sister T. M., 189
Hofer, Philip, 1043, 1044
Hoffman, D. G., 166
Hoffman, H., 1801
Hogan, Don, 764
Holland, Vyvyan, 1815, 1817, 1825, 1826
Hollis, Christopher, 1275
Holloway, H. A., 1150
Holloway, John, 93, 257, 516, 1342
Holloway, Sister M. M., 886
Holme, Thea, 494
Honan, Park, 356, 412, 413
Hone, J. M., 785
Hönnighausen, Gisela, 1372
Hood, T. L., 339
Hopkins, R. S., 645
Hopkins, R. T., 999
Hornbeck, B. G., 786
Hosmon, R. S., 1392
Hough, Graham, 94, 1208, 1314, 1502
Houghton, R. E., 258
Houghton, W. E., 95, 96, 167, 259, 607, 611, 975, 1276
House, Humphry, 858
Housman, Laurence, 939
Howard, R. R., 1430
Howe, Irving, 787, 788
Hubbell, G. S., 572
Hudson, Derek, 573, 574
Hudson, G. R., 347
Hudson, Ronald, 312
Hull, D. L., 646
Hunt, J. D., 1431, 1699, 1700
Hunt, Violet, 1403
Hunt, W. H., 1404
Hunter, Jim, 887
Huntley, J. F., 888
Huntley, W. B., 647
Hutton, R. H., 260, 261, 414, 612, 704, 1253, 1277, 1701
Huxley, Aldous, 976
Huxley, Julian, 959
Huxley, Leonard, 977, 978
Huxley, T. H., 648

INDEX

INDEX

INDEX

INDEX

INDEX